Do it  The Laz

MW00712637

1. Stock up on sale items. It saves on trips to the grocery.

2. Buy fresh ingredients that have already been diced, sliced, or otherwise prepared.

3. Teach your kids to help you in the kitchen.

4. You determine mealtimes and snack times and what's served.

5. Let your kids determine what and how much they eat.

*One luxurious
bubble bath*

*Access to most comfortable
chair and favorite TV show*

*One half-hour massage
(will need to recruit spouse, child, friend)*

*Time to recline and listen to a favorite CD
(or at least one song)*

cut

6. Serve a lot of fruits and vegetables—but don't force your kids to eat them.

7. Encourage your kids to stay active.

8. Offer your kids age-appropriate foods and servings.

9. When in doubt, serve noodles, rice, or bread.

10. Never say "never" to fun but "naughty" foods.

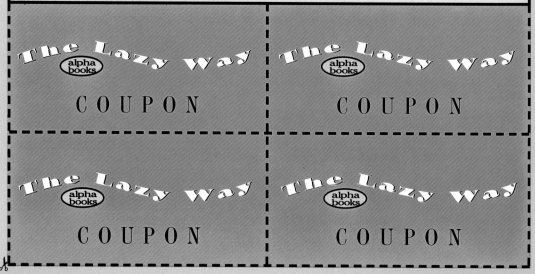

The Lazy Way

alpha
books

COUPON

The Lazy Way

alpha
books

COUPON

The Lazy Way

alpha
books

COUPON

The Lazy Way

alpha
books

COUPON

cut

Feed
Your Kids
Right

Feed Your Kids Right

Virginia Van Vynckt

The Lazy Way™

Macmillan • USA

To Lian and Daniel: Whatever would I do without you?

Copyright © 1999 Virginia Van Vynckt

All rights reserved. No part of this book shall be reproduced, stored in a retrieval system, or transmitted by any means, electronic, mechanical, photocopying, recording, or otherwise, without written permission from the publisher. No patent liability is assumed with respect to the use of the information contained herein. Although every precaution has been taken in the preparation of this book, the publisher and author assume no responsibility for errors or omissions. Neither is any liability assumed for damages resulting from the use of information contained herein. For information, address Alpha Books, 1633 Broadway, 7th Floor, New York, NY 10019-6785.

Macmillan Publishing books may be purchased for business or sales promotional use. For information please write: Special Markets Department, Macmillan Publishing USA, 1633 Broadway, New York, NY 10019.

International Standard Book Number: 0-02-863001-7
Library of Congress Catalog Card Number: 98-89489

01 00 99   8 7 6 5 4 3 2 1

Interpretation of the printing code: the rightmost number of the first series of numbers is the year of the book's printing; the rightmost number of the second series of numbers is the number of the book's printing. For example, a printing code of 99-1 shows that the first printing occurred in 1999.

Printed in the United States of America

Book Design: Madhouse Studios

Page Creation by David Faust and Heather Pope.

You Don't Have to Feel Guilty Anymore!

IT'S O.K. TO DO IT *THE LAZY WAY!*

It seems every time we turn around, we're given more responsibility, more information to absorb, more places we need to go, and more numbers, dates, and names to remember. Both our bodies and our minds are already on overload. And we know what happens next—cleaning the house, balancing the checkbook, and cooking dinner get put off until "tomorrow" and eventually fall by the wayside.

So let's be frank—we're all starting to feel a bit guilty about the dirty laundry, stacks of ATM slips, and Chinese takeout. Just thinking about tackling those terrible tasks makes you exhausted, right? If only there were an easy, effortless way to get this stuff done! (And done right!)

There is—*The Lazy Way*! By providing the pain-free way to do something—including tons of shortcuts and timesaving tips, as well as lists of all the stuff you'll ever need to get it done efficiently—*The Lazy Way* series cuts through all of the time-wasting thought processes and laborious exercises. You'll discover the secrets of those who have figured out *The Lazy Way*. You'll get things done in half the time it takes the average person—and then you will sit back and smugly consider those poor suckers who haven't discovered *The Lazy Way* yet. With *The Lazy Way,* you'll learn how to put in minimal effort and get maximum results so you can devote your attention and energy to the pleasures in life!

THE LAZY WAY PROMISE

Everyone on *The Lazy Way* staff promises that, if you adopt *The Lazy Way* philosophy, you'll never break a sweat, you'll barely lift a finger, you won't put strain on your brain, and you'll have plenty of time to put up your feet. We guarantee you will find that these activities are no longer hardships, since you're doing them *The Lazy Way*. We also firmly support taking breaks and encourage rewarding yourself (we even offer our suggestions in each book!). With *The Lazy Way*, the only thing you'll be overwhelmed by is all of your newfound free time!

THE LAZY WAY SPECIAL FEATURES

Every book in our series features the following sidebars in the margins, all designed to save you time and aggravation down the road.

- **"Quick n' Painless"**—shortcuts that get the job done fast.
- **"You'll Thank Yourself Later"**—advice that saves time down the road.
- **"A Complete Waste of Time"**—warnings that spare countless headaches and squandered hours.
- **"If You're So Inclined"**—optional tips for moments of inspired added effort.
- **"The Lazy Way"**—rewards to make the task more pleasurable.

If you've either decided to give up altogether or have taken a strong interest in the subject, you'll find information on hiring outside help with "How to Get Someone Else to Do It" as well as further reading recommendations in "If You Want to Learn More, Read These." In addition, there's an only-what-you-need-to-know glossary of terms and product names ("If You Don't Know What It Means/Does, Look Here") as well as "It's Time for Your Reward"—fun and relaxing ways to treat yourself for a job well done.

With *The Lazy Way* series, you'll find that getting the job done has never been so painless!

Series Editor
Amy Gordon

(signature: Amy Gordon)

Editorial Director
Gary Krebs

(signature: Gary Krebs)

Director of Creative Services
Michele Laseau

(signature: Michele Laseau)

Cover Designer
Michael Freeland

(signature: Michael J. Freeland)

Development Editor
Al McDermid

(signature: Al McDermid)

Production Editor
Christina Van Camp

(signature: Christina A. Van Camp)

What's in This Book

Real Food for Real Families

You know that soft drinks and fries aren't the cornerstones of good nutrition. You're alarmed when you offer your kids an apple and they stare at you as though you were the Wicked Queen in *Snow White.* In a previous, child-free life, you used to dust off a cookbook once in a while and make dinner. But now, after a day spent appeasing your irrational boss, drawing up home-school math lessons, or playing chauffeur to your daughter's soccer team, you just don't have the energy to make your son eat his green beans.

Relax. In this book, I share child- and parent-tested ways to get your kids to eat well without wearing them, or yourself, out with marathon cooking sessions or drawn-out food fights. After all, I've been there, done that.

People who know I'm a food writer sometimes remark how lucky my family is to have all those good meals. After I quit laughing, I explain that, except when someone's paying me, I spend little time in front of the stove. I have two wonderful children, Lian, food-lover and carnivore extraordinaire, and Daniel, the Carbo King, who could happily live on fruit, cookies, and french fries—when he bothers to eat. Then there's my husband, who's basically a meat-and-potatoes guy except that he likes spicy foods, which the kids won't eat. And me? If I had my druthers, I'd eat mostly a vegetarian diet with chocolate overtones.

This book is for people like you and me. We understand how important it is to feed our children well, and yet we need to juggle the schedules and tastes of a whole family without dropping the ball. We don't obsess about nutrition or gourmet fare, but we do know junky food from the good stuff. And we're not rich enough to routinely buy spa food carry-out or itty bitty carrot snack packs without thinking twice about the price.

Feed Your Kids Right The Lazy Way shows you how to stock your kitchen with the foods and tools you need for hassle-free meal preparation, and how to arrange it so it's kid-friendly and easier to clean. I share do-ahead tips that save you time in the long run, and provide instructions for making no-cook meals.

To help you wade effortlessly through the sea of nutrition information out there, I list the essential dos and don'ts of food safety and children's nutrition. In "Get Ready, Get Set..." and "No-Sweat Healthy Eating," you'll also learn how to plan headache-free menus, avoid power struggles at the table, and shop the supermarket without losing your kids or your sanity. You'll also find recipes and directions for making easy meals, divided by "lazy" strategy.

Numerous sidebars throughout the book explain quick and painless ways to perform tasks, suggest extra projects that might be fun to do, advise you on what you can do now to make your life easier later, warn against potential disasters, and share ideas for rewarding yourself and your kids for a job well done.

THANK YOU...

First, I owe a huge thank-you to Barbara Grunes, who supplied most of the recipes, plenty of helpful tips and, as always, an abundance of good cheer.

I'm grateful to Bev Bennett, Trish Maskew, Donna Clevenger, and Kristi Lubovich for sharing tips and experiences. For setting me straight on what kids like and don't like, I thank Lian and Daniel Weinstein, Rebecca and Ben Allen, Emma and Tess Sanders, Steven Ploense, Jessica Johnson, Carin Bridges, Marissa Grunes, and Meghan, Patrick, and Connor Maskew.

I thank Azriela Jaffe, author of *Honey, I Want To Start My Own Business: A Planning Guide For Couples,* for her humorous description of negotiating the supermarket with toddlers, which appeared in her e-mail newsletter, The Entrepreneurial Couples Success Letter.

I also applaud my husband, Marv Weinstein, for his patience and his willingness to make breakfast and lunch.

Finally, I thank my agent, Martha Casselman, for moral and hardware support, and my editors at Macmillan: Amy Gordon, for seeing the potential in this idea; Al McDermid, for shepherding it through development, and Christina Van Camp, for tweaking the copy into final form.

Obviously, I drew inspiration from numerous resources, printed and online, to complement my own experiences and ideas. Most are listed in "If You Really Want More, Read These," but I make special mention of Ellyn Satter's *How to Get Your Kid to Eat...But Not Too Much,* which has made mealtimes in so many households, including ours, more enjoyable.

Part 1

The Hassle-Free Kitchen

Are You Too Lazy to Read The Hassle-Free Kitchen?

1. The last time you saw your measuring spoons, your son, now a high school freshman, was in kindergarten. ☐ yes ☐ no

2. You finally mustered the ambition to whip up some homemade spaghetti sauce—and realized you're out of canned tomatoes. And tomato paste. And, uh-oh, spaghetti. ☐ yes ☐ no

3. If you've learned one thing from parenthood, it's that paper towels are essential to survival. But every time you rummage under the sink for them, the roll leaps out at you, then dances halfway across the kitchen. ☐ yes ☐ no

Taking Stock: Full Cupboards for Fast Meals

When you have what you need at the ready, preparing a meal or snack can be a snap. In fact, it can take far less time and effort than it does to detour to the fast-food restaurant, pick up dinner, and bring it home—all while trying to calm a car full of grumpy kids. And we won't even mention grumpy Mom or Dad.

Here are the foodstuffs and ingredients that I consider essential to a well-stocked kitchen. I'm listing only foods, including fresh ones, that keep for longer than a few days. Unless you have a farm, you'll still have to shop once a week or so for perishables. I'm also assuming you have the bare basics such as flour, salt, pepper, sugar, cooking oil, and at least a few herbs and spices.

QUICK ⬤ PAINLESS

My husband makes a super-quick tuna salad the kids love: water-packed tuna, drained and combined with enough Thousand Island dressing to moisten and flavor it. You can use low-fat dressing.

AT THE CORE: YOU CAN'T GO WRONG WITH THESE

These are the items that are always in my kitchen. With these on hand, I can toss together a meal, anytime, in no time flat. Add to this list as you like.

In the Cupboards or Pantry

- Canned chicken broth (preferably reduced-sodium).
- Canned crushed tomatoes. The crushed ones save a bit of time over the whole ones when you're making spaghetti sauce.
- Canned tomato paste.
- Canned tomato sauce.
- Bottled pasta sauce. For those times (maybe all the time) when you just don't have the energy to make spaghetti sauce yourself.
- Bottled salsa. Spoon it into or over everything from burritos to chili.
- Dry pasta and noodles. When you have kids, you can never have too many noodles in the house.
- Macaroni and cheese. It's neither health food nor gourmet fare, but I've yet to meet a kid who doesn't like it. It's quick, it's cheap, and you can make it lower in fat by using nonfat milk and less margarine. To ease guilt, serve it with cut-up raw fruits or veggies.
- Rice. Brown rice is richer in fiber and minerals; white rice is quicker. Converted rice, especially the boil-in-a-bag kind, tastes fine and is foolproof.

Tuna. Several cans. Water-packed, of course.

Canned and instant soups. I always keep the essential trio on hand: tomato, chicken noodle, and vegetable.

Beans. Open up a can of baked beans, heat them up, and you have a meal. Kidney or pinto beans are good in chili. Refried beans (low-fat) make a good spread or dip for tortillas, crackers, or corn chips. Chick-peas (garbanzos) taste great as is, or can be mushed into a dip.

Nonstick cooking spray. This lets you "fry" foods in very little fat.

Ketchup. Ask any kid; otherwise yucky foods can become quite tasty when drowned in ketchup.

Mayonnaise.

Peanut butter.

Jelly or jam. Seedless; kids don't like seeds (except for watermelon seeds, which they can spit at each other).

Cinnamon. Sprinkle it on toast, on hot cereal, or on anything your kids have a hankering for.

Vanilla. The real thing, please. Sprinkle into pancake batters, a bowl of cereal, or milk to boost its appeal.

Canned fruit and fruit juices.

Powdered or canned nonfat milk. For those out-of-milk emergencies, and to use as an ingredient in everything from breads to "cream" sauces.

IF YOU'RE SO
INCLINED

Freeze a 12- or 12.5-ounce can of guava nectar overnight. Let sit at room temperature for ten minutes, then remove the top of the can and spoon the "slushy" into two or three bowls. Guava is rich in vitamin C, and supplies iron and fiber.

YOU'LL THANK YOURSELF LATER

To freeze a whole package of meat, just put the whole store package in a large freezer bag, or wrap tightly in plastic wrap. The extra layer will protect it from freezer burn, and you'll be able to read through the plastic to see the label.

Cocoa mix and/or chocolate drink mix. This is how I coax my kids into drinking more milk.

Ready-to-eat cereal. Good for snacking as well as breakfast. Unsweetened cereals are best, but don't fret if you have sweetened ones on hand. As a snack, sweetened cereal still beats candy.

Hot cereals. I like good, old-fashioned oatmeal, but pick whatever your kids like. These are nutritious, warming, and filling. Don't overlook more offbeat choices, such as couscous (it's great for breakfast with a bit of cinnamon, sugar, and milk) or leftover rice (reheat it in a bit of milk, with a dash of sugar and cinnamon or vanilla).

Dried fruit. Apricots, raisins, and cherries are kid favorites.

Low-fat munchies. Pretzels, breadsticks, reduced-fat crackers, baked potato crisps, and low-fat croutons all "rotate" on my shelves.

Popcorn. As an ex-Hoosier (Indiana grows great popcorn), I favor the pop-your-own kind. But there's nothing wrong with a bagful of reduced-fat microwave popcorn. In fact, our family often makes a meal of popcorn and juice or fruit.

On the Counter

Garlic. Assuming your kids like it, that is. Of course, even if they don't, you usually can sneak a little into soups, spaghetti sauces, and such. I'm a stickler for fresh, but I promise not to tell if you use the bottled chopped stuff, or even—horrors—garlic powder.

Onions. Whole, if you don't mind chopping them yourself. But you can cop out and buy frozen chopped onions.

Potatoes. The bakers come in handy for a quick meal. Just toss them into the oven or zap them in the microwave, then spoon salsa, spaghetti sauce, or chili over them.

In the Freezer

Ground meat. White meat turkey is leanest, but if you really have to have beef in spaghetti sauce and the like, get ground round or sirloin.

Chicken breasts. The all-purpose white meat. They go with anything. Buy the boneless, skinless kind to save time; the kind with skin and bones for grilling.

Pork tenderloin. This is one of my favorite meats. It's lean, it tastes good, and it cooks quickly.

Lean beef. A good source of iron and zinc. To save time and effort, you can buy it already cut into strips or cubes for stir-fries and stews.

Frozen vegetables. I always try to keep peas, corn, and spinach on hand.

Bread. If you've got kids, you'd better have an extra loaf or two hanging around.

Tortillas. They take only seconds to thaw in the microwave, and you can wrap all kinds of things in them.

Ready-made pizza crusts. Why not just buy frozen pizzas? Because so many are loaded with cheese

IF YOU'RE SO
INCLINED

When you buy a cut-up chicken, save the necks and backs. Do the same with vegetable scraps, such as potato and carrot peelings. Bring a pot of water to a boil, toss in the frozen scraps, and simmer for a couple of hours to make a delicious broth.

IF YOU'RE SO
INCLINED

Give juice a fizzy pick-me-up: Let the kids scoop 2 tablespoons of frozen apple, grape, or orange juice concentrate into a tall glass, fill with soda water and ice cubes, then stir.

and/or meat, and you need a microscope to find any veggies besides the sauce. You can top a ready-made crust with whatever vegetables your kids like, and keep the cheese to a reasonable amount. The crusts come plain or packaged with sauce.

- Frozen waffles.

- Orange juice. There's no easier way to get a day's vitamin C. We like the pasteurized juice, but keep frozen concentrate on hand as "insurance."

- Frozen juice bars. They're not nutritional power-houses, but they help kids get enough liquid when they've been out playing on a hot day.

In the Fridge

- Yogurt (nonfat or low-fat).

- Apples. Unlike many fruits, apples should be refrigerated. Keep them in the crisper drawer and set the humidity control to low.

- Juice.

- Milk. Nonfat or reduced-fat, or as we used to say in the olden days, skim, 1 percent, or 2 percent. If your children are under the age of 1, stick to formula or breast milk. If under the age of 2, serve them whole milk. If your child is allergic to dairy or doesn't tolerate it well, or if you prefer not to drink milk, stock up on calcium-fortified rice or soy drink.

- Carrots. Buy the prewashed baby carrots for less fuss.

- Bag of slaw. Either the broccoli kind or the cabbage variety. Besides making quick coleslaw, these also are great to toss into soups or stir-fries.
- Celery sticks. A lot of kids like the crunch, and they go great with peanut butter.
- Cream cheese. I buy the reduced-fat kind.
- Salad dressings. Preferably low-fat or nonfat. These are useful for a lot more than dressing lettuce. You can use them to marinate meat, poultry, and fish. Or dump them over cooked vegetables for an instant flavor boost.
- Eggs. Although they are indeed high in cholesterol (more than 200 milligrams of the stuff in one egg), eggs have several virtues: Most kids like them, they're cheap, and they're really versatile.
- Hard cheeses. They help clean kids' teeth and are rich in calcium. They are high in fat, so use them in moderation, or get the reduced-fat varieties. There are also a number of fat-free "cheeses," but personally, I'd rather my kids nibble on erasers (which, come to think of it, they do).
- Mozzarella. For pizzas.

NOT ESSENTIAL, BUT KIDS LIKE 'EM

These items don't belong to my "core" collection, but do pop up frequently in my kitchen.

In the Cupboards or Pantry

- Low-fat cookies such as fig-filled bars, graham crackers, animal crackers, biscotti…anything that falls into

QUICK ⬛ PAINLESS

Some baking recipes call for fruit puree, usually apricots or prunes, to replace some or all of the fat. You can buy fruit puree in the supermarket's baking aisle. Or just use apricot or prune baby food, which costs less and comes in smaller jars.

the "treat" category without being outrageously fatty or sugar-laden. Whole grain is even better.

- Baking mix. A quick way to whip up pancakes, biscuits, shortcakes, and whatever else.
- Applesauce. Besides being a good snack, it also can be used as a partial fat replacer in baked goods. It also tastes great with hash browns for breakfast.
- Honey. Sweetens things naturally, and is great mixed in hot water as a throat-coater when your kid has a cold.

In the Fridge

- Refrigerated biscuits or rolls. They're not only good as the bread side, but can serve as crusts for a whole bunch of other things, such as pizza. Whole wheat biscuits and rolls are nice, and might appeal to the kids more than whole wheat bread.

In the Freezer

- Fruit. Berries and peaches are wonderful to have when summer is but a memory.
- Frozen potatoes. While I prefer my potatoes fresh, these products can be real time-savers. The frozen hash browns have no fat, and taste like fresh.
- Stuffed dumplings or pasta. Tortellini and ravioli are available in supermarkets. Asian food markets (and some supermarkets) carry frozen gyoza or pot stickers (dumplings). They aren't necessarily low in fat, but they're nutritious and make good, quick meals. Brown them in a skillet and serve them with

YOU'LL THANK YOURSELF LATER

What about high-fat but tasty foods, such as regular hot dogs or premium ice cream? It's easier to resist them if you rarely keep them in the house. When you crave fried chicken or french fries, grab the kids and go out for them.

ketchup or sweet and sour sauce. Boil them and serve them in spaghetti sauce. Dump them into boiling chicken broth, toss in some vegetables, and yell, "Soup's on!"

GIVE THEM A TRY

These are foods that may or may not have ever seen the inside of your kitchen, but that are healthful and appeal to a lot of kids.

- Bottled water. Essential if you're not fond of your tap water (or don't trust it!). Kids are also more likely to think water is special if it comes out of a bottle.

- Tofu. It's rich in protein, and very versatile. Whirl the soft kind with fruits to make shakes. Firm tofu is a good binder, and can substitute for eggs in some recipes. I sometimes scramble it 50-50 with eggs.

- Veggie burgers. Some are quite tasty, all are significantly lower in saturated fat than their beefier cousins, and they're a good way to "sneak" veggies into a meal. You'll never know whether your kids like them if you don't serve them.

Just returned from a marathon shopping expedition? Once you've put the groceries away, sit down, put your feet up, and read your kids a favorite book. Or have them read one to you.

The Lazy Way

Getting Time on Your Side

	The Old Way	The Lazy Way
Making tuna salad	5 minutes	2 minutes
Making hash browns	30 minutes	10 minutes
Grating cabbage for slaw	10 minutes	0 minutes
Making sorbet or slushies	$2\frac{1}{2}$ hours	2 hours
Making dumplings	2 hours	10 minutes
Making pizza crust	$1\frac{1}{2}$ hours	0 hours

two

Labor-Saving Tools for Peace of Mind

OK, I admit it. I used to make "boutique" style breads from scratch. I nursed sourdoughs, studied flour composition, and fretted over loaves that turned out not quite right. I had a bread machine, but used it maybe a couple of times a year.

Now I live at 5,000 feet, where doughs collapse. I have to drive to the next town for good bakery bread. I juggle a sometimes hectic schedule. Most important, I have two kids, who think bread is its own food group.

I now use the bread machine a couple of times a week.

Like many of the tools I feature in this chapter, bread machines aren't essential. They sure do make life easier, though.

Here, I list some of the tools, large and small, that I view as "musts." I've specifically included items that make working in the kitchen easier for parents, as opposed to normal people.

MEAN MACHINES: APPLIANCES, LARGE AND SMALL

Whatever did people do before the invention of electricity? Here are my winners in the plug-it-in-and-go category.

Dishwasher

There are three great scientific achievements of the 20th century: the Theory of Relativity, the computer, and the dishwasher. If you don't already own a dishwasher, consider begging, borrowing, or stealing the space for one. This is especially urgent if you have ever-snacking toddlers or teens.

Choosing a dishwasher isn't too hard. After all, we're basically talking about a machine that squirts hot water and soap. Most mid-priced models ($300 to $500) do a good job. Do avoid the bargain-basement models. Here's what you need:

- Three cycles (light, normal, heavy). Ninety-nine percent of the time, you'll use the normal cycle. A rinse-and-hold cycle comes in handy if it takes you more than a couple of days to build up a full load—not likely with kids in the house.

- One that's easy to load and unload. Some of this depends on personal preference and the type of dishes you wash most often.

- Disposer. It grinds up and disposes of soft pieces of food, so you don't have to be as scrupulous about scraping plates.

A COMPLETE WASTE OF TIME

The 3 Worst Things to Put in a Dishwasher:

1. Your wooden salad bowl. It can crack.

2. Glass jars with labels. They gum up the works.

3. Dinner. Forget "recipes" for steaming fish in the machine.

Bread Machine

Ah, the joy of measuring flour, water, and yeast into a pan, then walking away. A bonus to bread machines is that any kid who can measure and push a button can make bread.

If you plan to buy a bread machine, here are features I recommend beyond the basics, which usually include a whole wheat cycle, dough cycle, and delay-start timer:

- Cooling fan. This way, you don't even have to set the delay-start timer. Just start the machine before you go to sleep or off to work. The cooling cycle will keep the baked bread from getting soggy as it sits in the enclosure.

- French bread cycle. I use this cycle all the time because it yields the crispest crust.

- Sweet bread cycle. This allows for the longer rising times that work best with doughs that are high in sugar.

- Programmable mode. A nicety that allows you to "tweak" things by adjusting the kneading, rising, and baking cycles.

Microwave Ovens

You probably already have one. But do you use it for anything other than reheating foods or popping corn? In a microwave, you can prepare entire meals in no time at all. It's especially good at steaming things, such as vegetables.

If you're planning to replace your microwave, your best bet is probably a family-sized one (1.1 to 1.39 cubic

IF YOU'RE SO INCLINED

Want to make bread from scratch? Dough rises quickly in a microwave's small space. Warm it by heating a glass measuring cup of water on "high" until boiling. Remove the cup, put the bowl of dough in the microwave, and shut the door (don't turn the oven on).

feet), which is large and powerful enough to handle most meals without requiring a room of its own. Other than that, look for:

- Ease of use. You want plenty of one-step buttons for such functions as defrosting, reheating a plate of food, popping popcorn, or cooking potatoes. You also want to be able to program the thing without needing a master's degree.

- Moisture sensor. Senses when a food is done. It takes a lot of the guesswork out of cooking and reheating.

- Child lockout. Nearly all ovens have these; you just punch in a code to make the microwave off limits.

When you do get your oven, read the instruction booklet. Once you learn how to program various cooking times and levels, you and your kids can use your oven to do everything from melting chocolate to steaming fish.

If you have preschool or younger children, keep the microwave out of their reach or use that lockout feature. The last thing you need is your 3-year-old zapping his rubber bath toys. For older children, however, the microwave is a blessing. It's easy to use (with parental supervision, of course), and the interior doesn't heat up, making it safer than a regular oven.

Toaster Oven

Even—and maybe especially—if you heat up your regular oven only when the moon is full and Gemini is rising, you'll want a toaster oven for all those little jobs, from heating up leftover pizza to, well, making toast.

QUICK ⬤ PAINLESS

Do you still have problems programming the microwave's time and cook cycles? Ask your kid how to do it. After all, didn't she teach you how to program the VCR and use the computer?

Actually, a regular toaster makes better toast, but you can't stick pita pizzas in it.

Older children can use a toaster oven, with less risk of getting burned than when they use a full-size oven.

Toaster ovens are pretty basic, but look for these features:

- Ease of cleaning. Some have a pop-open bottom tray, but I prefer the ones with a crumb tray that pulls out so you can plop it in the sink. Look for an easy-to-clean, nonstick interior surface.

- A cavity that's at least 11 inches wide and 9 inches deep, so it will hold four slices of toast in a single layer. Manufacturers often claim that smaller ovens hold four slices. I guess they mean Melba toast. Take a ruler with you.

Blender

How else are you going to make milk shakes and breakfast smoothies?

The instruction booklet that comes with your blender will extol its virtues in doing everything from chopping to grinding. But it really works best for liquids.

When buying a blender, your main choice is which style you prefer: regular, in which the container sits atop a motorized base, or handheld (immersion), in which the motor sits atop a shaft and blade assembly that you put into the container of food. The latter is more versatile, but the regular styles tend to have more power, and their containers hold more liquid.

YOU'LL THANK YOURSELF LATER

When you or the kids toast anything greasy (such as pita pizzas) in the toaster oven, use the tray provided, and clean it afterward. Doing so will help prevent grease fires.

GET IT TOGETHER: ORGANIZERS

Having the right tools in the right place saves time you would otherwise spend hunting down this and that or thinning out the accumulating piles on your counter. Here's what I recommend:

- Magnets. What's the difference between a child-free house and one with kids? You can see the front of the refrigerator in the child-free house. So figure on having magnets. Lots of magnets.

- Wipe-off board and erasable marker. Because the kitchen is the heart of most homes, it's often "message central." We use a wipe-off board to keep track of appointments, reminders, messages, and shopping lists.

- Hard plastic pockets for papers. You'll find these in office-supply and discount stores. They're either magnetic or they attach to a wall or cupboard. I use three: a small one for coupons, and two larger ones—one for restaurant take-out menus and school papers and another for loose recipes. You can also attach one to the inside of a cupboard door to store the lids to all those plastic containers that somehow keep breeding in your cupboards.

- See-through plastic bins. These can help organize small foods (like packets of spices) and snacks—have a couple of bins in the refrigerator or cupboard with "approved" foods from which kids can help themselves. If your child has food allergies, assemble a bin of foods that are safe for her to eat.

IF YOU'RE SO
INCLINED

You may want to install the ideal kitchen "appliance," a cordless phone. Inevitably, someone calls when you're preparing dinner. And no cords means you can follow the kids around the house (or escape from them) as you talk.

- Pullout baskets. Ever noticed how kids can never find anything if it's not staring them in the face? Actually, I have the same problem. With pullout baskets installed in our cupboards, the kids and I can find the spaghetti sauce even if it's lurking behind the croutons.

- Paper towel holder. Install it near the sink. And by the way, always buy paper towels in bulk; you'll never have enough.

- Knife block or magnetized strip. Keep it well away from the front of the counter, where a young child can't reach it. If you have an adventurous climber, lock the knives away.

SMALL BUT MIGHTY MISCELLANY

Even if you don't cook much, you probably own basic cookware and utensils. But here are some parent-specific needs.

- Measuring cups and spoons. You'll want two 2-cup liquid measures: one in glass, which can take hot liquids, and one in plastic, which your kids can use. Get two sets each of dry measuring cups and measuring spoons, as insurance against the day when your kids borrow them for the teddy bears' tea party.

- Vegetable peeler. It's easier to use than a knife, and safer for kids, who can peel their own carrots.

- Scissors. For slicing open food packages and cutting dried bread dough out of your son's hair.

QUICK ⬛ PAINLESS

Buy plastic cups in different bright colors, and "assign" a certain color or colors to each child. That will end any confusion about whose juice is whose.

- Unbreakable cups. Since glasses can slip so easily out of children's fingers, these are a must.

- Cookie cutters. Even if you don't make cookies, you'll be cutting foods into shapes. Dinosaur sandwiches, anyone?

BETTER SAFE THAN SORRY

If you have children, safety in the kitchen is extremely important. Here are some areas to watch out for.

The Obvious Stuff

- Poisons. These include such items as cleaning supplies, dishwasher soap (which includes bleach), and vitamins. Keep them well out of reach and locked up.

- Locks. Child safety locks will keep toddlers out of cupboards. Once the kid is old enough to figure out how to undo them, "out of sight out of mind" works best. If you have an older child who's curious, keep the cleaning supplies and other dangerous goods locked up with a combination padlock.

- The stove. Most electric stoves have the controls at the rear, and modern gas stoves have safety knobs that you have to push in and turn. If you have an old gas stove, remove the knobs when you're not cooking and keep them out of the kids' reach. When you're cooking, turn pot handles inward, away from the edge of the stove, so a curious child can't grab the pot.

YOU'LL THANK YOURSELF LATER

People always remember to keep potholders by the stove, but do you have a pair by the microwave? The oven itself may not heat up, but the foods and dishes inside it do.

Have You Thought of These?

- Canned goods. They can hurt little toes and fingers if they're dropped—not to mention the dent they make in the refrigerator when your 2-year-old decides to practice her pitching skills with the baked beans.

- Cords. Toddlers have strangled on telephone cords. Make sure all phone and appliance cords are out of reach of little hands. Another rule of thumb: If your kids are old enough to reach appliances but not old enough to use them safely, keep them unplugged when they're not in use (the appliances, that is).

So, you've finally equipped your kitchen the way you want. Have a slice of bread warm from the bread-maker—and spread on some of that fancy jam you've hidden from the children.

The Lazy Way

Getting Time on Your Side

	The Old Way	The Lazy Way
Kneading bread dough	10 minutes	Machine does it
Washing dishes	15 minutes	Machine does it
Steaming vegetables	10 minutes	2 to 3 minutes
Arguing over whose cup is whose	10 minutes	Won't happen
Finding the paper towels	2 minutes	30 seconds
Searching for lids	3 minutes	30 seconds

Part 2

The Express Lane

Are You Too Lazy to Read The Express Lane?

1 Yes, you heard the alarm. But the thought of trying to pack three school lunches while you make breakfast has you hiding your head under the covers. ☐ yes ☐ no

2 It's too hot to heat up the stove. You're too tired to go out to eat, and your fairy godmother is taking the day off. ☐ yes ☐ no

3 It's not that you're a lousy housekeeper or anything. But your kitchen could star in its own horror movie. ☐ yes ☐ no

A Chop in Time Saves Nine

Why put off till tomorrow what you can do today? Just a bit of extra effort will pay off handsomely a day, a week, or even a month from now. My do-ahead strategies boil down to three categories:

- Getting a head start on tomorrow's tasks while you're in the kitchen today,

- Preparing ingredients before you start cooking, and

- Buying or preparing more than you need so you'll have extras to use later.

WHILE YOU'RE IN THE KITCHEN

When are you more likely to remember to pull tomorrow's chicken out of the freezer and put it in the refrigerator to thaw? When you're cleaning up after tonight's dinner? Or tomorrow morning, when you're trying to get the kids off to school without losing their mittens, their lunches, or your mind?

QUICK **n** PAINLESS

Toss bananas that are getting overripe into the freezer, peel and all. To make yummy breakfast shakes, thaw the frozen bananas for 5 minutes, cut off the peel, and cut them into chunks. Whirl in a blender with milk or orange juice.

Rise and Shine

You've probably read those studies reporting that kids do better in school when they eat breakfast. But c'mon, who has time to deal with a meal when you're still groggy? So, deal with it the night before, while you're still awake:

- If you have a breadmaker, pop the ingredients into it just before going to bed. Set the timer for the wee hours of the morning so you can wake up to freshly baked bread. Warning: Do NOT program it ahead if you're making dough with fresh milk and/or egg in it; they should not sit out for several hours before baking.

- Set the table with the bowls and spoons for cereal, and set out the cereal boxes or packets.

- Planning to make scrambled eggs or omelets? Crack the eggs into a bowl, add salt and pepper, and refrigerate. In the morning, all you have to do is whisk and cook.

- Pour juice into the kids' glasses and put them in the fridge.

- For breakfast smoothies, cut up the fruit the night before, and put it and the milk, yogurt, or juice in the blender container, put the lid on, and refrigerate the whole bit.

- If you're planning to make pancakes, measure the dry ingredients into a bowl and leave it on the counter. Mix the egg, milk, and oil together in a measuring cup and pop them into the refrigerator. In the morning, just whisk the two mixtures together.

And for the Rest of the Day...

- If you're going to have meat or chicken for tomorrow night's dinner, take it out of the freezer and put it in the refrigerator just after tonight's dinner.

- If there's a stir-fry in your near future, chop up the vegetables the night before and put them in resealable bags in the refrigerator.

- Stick juice boxes in the freezer to put in your children's lunch the next day. They'll help keep foods cold and will still be nice and chilly when lunchtime rolls around.

- If it's summer, fill the kids' water bottles up halfway, then freeze overnight. In the morning, you can fill them up the rest of the way so the kids will have chilled water.

Now that You're Home from the Store

The best time to prepare ahead is right after you come home from the supermarket. After all, everything is there, right in front of you. All you have to do is spend a few minutes separating stuff to make your life for the coming week so much easier.

- Buy in bulk when things are on sale. Whether it's baby food or chicken breasts, buy as much as you have room to store. Although it's more immediate work to put the stuff away or divide it up, in the long run it means fewer trips to the supermarket.

YOU'LL THANK YOURSELF LATER

Always make kids' school lunches the night before. They'll be ready to go in the morning, and if you make them after the kids are asleep, you don't have to listen to, "Aw, Mom, I already had peanut butter sandwiches this week."

- If you buy bulk snacks such as granola, sunflower seeds, pretzels, cereal, snack crackers or dried fruit for lunches, separate them into individual servings and store them in sandwich bags, to be pulled out as needed.

- Likewise, as soon as you come home from the grocery store, cut up raw vegetables and fruits (if they're already ripe) to make a week's worth of snacks. Put them in tightly sealed storage bags and keep them in a "snack bin" in the refrigerator.

- Trying to pry apart frozen meats is no fun. If you've bought large packages of meat or poultry on sale, now's the time to separate them into meal-size packages, or to cut them up for stews or stir-fries.

THINK LIKE A CHEF

No, that doesn't mean you have to serve the kids smoked salmon on a bed of organic field greens with essence of wild leek. (Although you can if you want to; just call and let me know when dinner will be served.) It does mean that it pays to prepare ingredients ahead of time. In a restaurant, the tomatoes are chopped, the garlic is minced, and the salad greens are washed before the doors even open for dinner. (Of course, your favorite chef also has sous chefs, or assistants, to do these tasks. So do you. They're called children and spouses.)

Seasoned Express

- Puerto Rican cooks call it *sofrito,* a seasoning mixture. Likewise, if there's a certain combination of

QUICK n' PAINLESS

Cutting up beef or pork for use later in stir-fries? Stick the meat in the freezer for an hour, or until frozen but not solid. It'll slice like a dream.

seasoning ingredients you tend to cook with over and over again—for example, a mixture of peppers and onions, or minced garlic and ginger for stir-fries—cook up a big batch. Remove it to a plate to cool, divide up into small freezer bags, and freeze.

- Keep cinnamon sugar on hand. Mix 1/2 cup sugar with 1 tablespoon ground cinnamon, and store in an airtight container. It's great for cinnamon toast, to sprinkle on cereal, and to flavor fruit that needs a little boost of sweetness.

- Season foods ahead of time. When you're dividing chicken or meat up into packages for the freezer, sprinkle it with your favorite seasonings: Cajun, Italian herbs, lemon pepper, whatever you like. Do be aware that salt can dry out foods and make them go rancid faster. If you plan to freeze the meat for more than a couple of weeks, it's best to use salt-free seasoning mixes.

Mix It, Wash It, Peel It Today

- If you have a favorite baking recipe you make over and over again, mix up the dry ingredients (for example, flour, sugar, salt, and yeast or baking powder) in the proper proportions, and store in resealable freezer bags or airtight containers on the shelf. If you don't plan to use them within a month or so, store them in the freezer. Let the mixes come to room temperature before using them.

YOU'LL THANK YOURSELF LATER

Take the crusts you've trimmed from bread, or the "heels" your kids won't eat, and let them sit out on the counter until dry and crunchy. Whirl in a blender or food processor to make bread crumbs. Store in an airtight container.

To keep foods such as raw vegetables fresher longer, put them in a resealable storage bag and stick a straw about halfway into the bag, at one corner. Seal the bag shut up to the straw. Suck out as much air as you can. Remove the straw and zip the bag shut. Warning: Only do this with foods you can safely eat uncooked.

- Wash and separate the leaves in a head of lettuce ahead of time. Place them in a resealable plastic storage bag with a dry paper towel or two (to absorb excess moisture), then squeeze out as much air as possible (use the straw trick), and return to the crisper drawer.

- Chopping up garlic for your sauce? Chop up an extra clove or two and mash it with a ½ cup (1 stick) of softened butter or margarine. When you want garlic bread, just thaw the mixture and spread it on French or Italian bread.

BUY NOW, MAKE NOW, ENJOY LATER

Those extra chopped onions will come in oh-so-handy next week when you've promised your kids homemade spaghetti sauce and you're so tired you can barely lift a pot.

Put It on Ice

- Open a big can of chicken broth, and pour any you're not using now into small containers or ice cube trays. One ice cube compartment equals about 2 tablespoons of broth.

- Buy a bunch of basil, parsley, cilantro, or other herbs. Use what you need, then chop up the rest and measure a tablespoonful into each compartment of an ice cube tray. Moisten with a bit of water, then freeze to add later to dishes such as spaghetti sauce, soup, or even salsa and pesto.

Next time lemons or limes are on sale (or the back-yard tree is full), squeeze a bunch of them and pour the juice into ice cube trays. Freeze and use in recipes as needed. One cubeful equals about 2 table-spoons.

Making frosting for your daughter's birthday cake, and your son's birthday's just around the corner? Make a double batch, and freeze the rest. Butter- or shortening-based frostings will keep well in the freezer for up to six months.

Buy a whole bunch of English muffins or pita breads, top each with a smear of sauce and grated cheese, and freeze. For a snack or light lunch, your kids can retrieve them from the freezer and heat them up in the toaster oven or even the microwave.

If you're chopping one onion, you might as well chop three. Freeze the extra, to use later in any cooked dish. The bonus of chopping up several onions is that it gives you an incentive to use the food chopper or food processor, saving even more time.

To freeze small pieces of food (such as raspber-ries or chopped onions), spread them out in a single layer on a cookie sheet. Freeze until solid, then spoon the frozen bits into freezer bags. Seal the bags and return the food to the freezer.

If you're making rice, toss an extra cupful or two into the pot. Let the extra rice cool, then put in an airtight container or freezer bag, and freeze. Next

QUICK ⏱ PAINLESS

Going out to eat tonight? Order tomorrow night's dinner (or at least part of it) as well: an extra order of steamed rice, a couple of extra orders of french fries, some stir-fried veg-etables—whatever you can get to go.

While you're at the supermarket, pick up healthy, "exotic" desserts, such as fresh figs, fresh lychees, cherimoya, starfruit, or a new apple variety. Once you're relaxing after dinner, you and the kids can enjoy a fruit tasting.

The Lazy Way

time you need a quick meal, toss the frozen rice in a skillet or wok with oil, some bits of meat and vegetables, a little soy sauce, some garlic and ginger, and voilà—fried rice.

- Cooking pasta? Toss a couple of extra handfuls into the pot. Toss the extras with a bit of oil, put in an airtight container, and refrigerate. You can even freeze it for a short period (about a couple of weeks max).

- At the height of tomato season, buy a bunch at the farmers market. Bring a big pot of water to a boil and toss them in for 30 seconds. Remove the tomatoes, and as soon as they're cool enough to handle, slip off the peels (if the fruit is ripe, the peels should come right off). Pack the peeled tomatoes into freezer containers or bags, and freeze to make sauces later.

- If you're ambitious enough to cook dried beans from scratch, make more than you'll need. Toss the remainder with just a bit of oil, and freeze.

- Next time you make a batch of cookies, immediately put some in a tin and freeze them. That way the kids (and you) won't be as tempted to eat them all at once, and you'll have some cookies squirreled away for the next time you feel like having them. Let them thaw at room temperature.

Getting Time on Your Side

	The Old Way	The Lazy Way
Defrosting the chicken for dinner	10 minutes	Already done
Getting breakfast ready in the morning	20 minutes	5 to 10 minutes
Freezing small foods	1 hour	30 minutes
Chopping veggies for tonight's stir-fry	20 minutes	Already done
Packing snacks for tomorrow's lunch	5 minutes	Already done
Seasoning chicken for dinner tonight	5 to 10 minutes	Already done

Chapter four

Assembly Only Required

Add a waiter or two, and your average supermarket could pass for a restaurant these days. The collection of heat-and-eat, or don't-even-bother-to-heat, foods is enormous.

Here's just a sampling of what you'll find in the average supermarket: roast chicken, fried chicken, potato salad, coleslaw, three-bean salad, carrot salad, fresh salsa, relish trays, sandwiches, complete lunches to go, heat-them-up entrees, precut raw vegetables, various slaws and salads in bags (with or without dressing), bottled mangos and papayas, ready-made dips and sauces, bottled minced garlic and ginger, cut-up fresh fruits, cooked crab (real and mock), cooked shrimp, tuna salad in a can, ready-to-eat puddings, and cheese and crackers.

In a pinch, you can buy everything ready-made and just open packages, but for more interesting fare, buy the components and assemble them in new combinations. Here's a collection of meals that require no cooking or real preparation,

A COMPLETE WASTE OF TIME

The 3 Worst Things to Do with Pizza:

1. Microwave it. Talk about glue...

2. Drown it in cheese. Sorry, all you Chicagoans out there.

3. Order or buy it with three different kinds of fatty meats, as though sausage or pepperoni alone didn't have enough fat.

or that require so little of either that the time spent is negligible.

Note that I don't include amounts of ingredients, or serving yields. I want you to feel free to adjust the ingredients and amounts to your family's taste.

SALADS IN A SNAP

You probably think of salads as collections of leafy greens, with maybe a tomato or two. Here are some ideas to help you expand that definition.

Shrimp and Tropical Fruit Salad

This salad is most likely to appeal to older kids, although younger ones can pick out the fruit, shrimp or lettuce—whichever they like to eat. It makes a nice lunch or light dinner. Accompany it with plenty of bread.

A head of Bibb or Boston lettuce

Sliced mangos or papayas (from a jar), drained

Precooked shrimp

A fairly sweet vinaigrette-style salad dressing (such as balsamic or raspberry vinaigrette, or poppyseed dressing)

Salt and pepper

1 Wash the lettuce and separate it into leaves.

2 Arrange the lettuce on a large platter.

3 Arrange the mangos in a circle atop the lettuce leaves.

4 Mound the shrimp in the middle.

5 Drizzle the dressing over the salad, and sprinkle lightly with salt and pepper. Serve this salad with bread or cooked rice.

QUICK ⦿ PAINLESS

To easily remove the core from a head of lettuce, pick up the lettuce, with the core on the bottom, and thump it down on the counter or cutting board. This will loosen the core so you can just pull it out.

YOU'LL THANK YOURSELF LATER

When you buy a rotis-
serie chicken in the deli,
buy a couple of extra
ones. Bring them home,
pull off the meat, and
freeze extras for future
meals.

Chinese-Style Chicken Salad

You can give your children a food history lesson with this one:
Tangerines are named for Tangiers, in Morocco. And when
they ask you where Morocco is, be sure you know.

Deli roast chicken

Seedless tangerines (Clementines) (or canned mandarin
    oranges, drained)

Small can of whole or sliced water chestnuts

Roasted almonds

Green onions (optional)

Vinaigrette-style dressing with soy and/or ginger in it

1   Separate the chicken into small serving pieces. Arrange
    them on a platter.

2   Peel the tangerines and separate them into sections.
    Scatter the tangerine sections around the chicken.

3   Drain the water chestnuts and scatter them around the
    chicken as well.

4   Coarsely chop the almonds and, if desired, green onions,
    and sprinkle both over the chicken, tangerines, and water
    chestnuts.

5   Drizzle the dressing over the salad. This is great with left-
    over rice, if you have any on hand.

Turkey Caesar

There's no reason not to serve this easy restaurant favorite at home. For the best flavor, use fresh Parmesan cheese, not the dried shelf-stable stuff.

Romaine lettuce mix

Sliced roasted turkey breast, or chicken

Grated fresh Parmesan cheese

Seasoned croutons

Caesar-style salad dressing

1   Place the lettuce in a large bowl.

2   Shred the sliced turkey and add it to the lettuce.

3   Add the cheese and croutons; toss thoroughly.

4   Add enough dressing to moisten and toss again. Serve this with fruit and bread.

QUICK ⬛ PAINLESS

One of the favorite summer main courses at our house is cooked pasta tossed with finely chopped almonds (preferably roasted), lots of finely chopped basil, and some olive oil and grated Parmesan. Toss in a little chopped garlic if your kids like it.

IF YOU'RE SO
INCLINED

To whip up your own coleslaw dressing, mix $^1/_2$ cup mayonnaise with 2 tablespoons of cider vinegar and 1 tablespoon of sugar. Add a sprinkling of celery seed if you like.

Fall Turkey and Veggie Salad

Broccoli slaw or cabbage slaw (in a bag)

Roasted turkey breast (not sliced)

Gala or Fuji apples

Coleslaw dressing

1 Place the slaw in a large bowl.

2 Cut the turkey into chunks. Add to the slaw and toss.

3 Cut the apples in half, remove the cores, and cut the apples into chunks. Toss with the turkey and slaw.

4 Add dressing to taste, and toss again.

5 This is good with rye bread or rolls.

Tuna and Vegetable Plate

This is very loosely inspired by salade Niçoise, a favorite in southern France.

Potato salad

Green bean salad or three-bean salad (from the deli)

Water-packed albacore tuna

Vinaigrette-style dressing of your choice

Marinated artichoke hearts (optional)

Cherry tomatoes

1 Place scoops of potato salad and bean salad on a platter.

2 Drain the tuna and toss it with enough dressing to moisten it.

3 Scatter the tuna, artichoke hearts, and cherry tomatoes around the potato salad and bean salad. Serve with plenty of bread.

YOU'LL THANK YOURSELF LATER

Teach your children—and yourself—to put canned tuna into a sieve to drain it. Pressing the cut lid against the tuna to drain off the liquid makes it too easy to cut your fingers.

Save some of those cones for dessert, too. Wouldn't a bit of fudge ripple ice cream or frozen yogurt hit the spot?

The Lazy Way

Salads in Cones

Kids love offbeat ideas, like serving foods in unexpected containers.

Deli salads of your choice, such as tuna salad, chicken salad, carrot salad, coleslaw, pasta salad, potato salad

Small ice cream cones (plain style, not sugar)

1 Let the children pick out which salads they like, and put a scoop or two of each salad in a cone.

2 Serve, with spoons for "backup."

Italian-Style Bean and Tomato Salad

Although sage is traditional in this salad, most kids prefer basil, which is not as pungent.

Canned cannelloni or Great Northern beans

Fresh tomatoes

Fresh basil or sage

Olive oil

Fresh clove(s) of garlic, smashed (optional)

1 Drain the beans, rinse them, drain again, and put in a bowl.

2 Coarsely chop the tomatoes. Add to the beans.

3 Chop up the basil or sage. Add to the beans.

4 Drizzle the olive oil over the salad. Add the garlic, if desired, and gently toss.

5 Serve with plenty of Italian bread.

QUICK ⬭ PAINLESS

To chop basil easily, roll the leaves up into a tight cylinder, then cut into thin slices. This is known as chiffonade.

QUICK **n** PAINLESS

Fresh figs are wonderful, but if they're not in season, use dried figs. If you like, you can plump them by submerging them briefly in boiling water, then draining them.

Melon, Figs, and Ham

Cut-up melon (different varieties)

Fresh figs

Lean ham, preferably turkey ham

Breadsticks

1 Roll up the ham into cylinders.

2 Mound the melon in the center of the plate.

3 Surround the melon with the figs, the ham cylinders, and the breadsticks.

SUDDENLY SANDWICHES

Sandwiches rank as popular meals with all ages. Here are a few that go beyond the usual turkey-mayo combo.

Southwestern Beef Rolls

This is a roast beef sandwich with a little more zip. If your kids don't favor peppers, you can substitute lettuce.

Hard rolls

Thinly sliced roast beef from the deli

Roasted peppers (you might want to use sweet red peppers for the kids, roasted chiles for the adults)

Mayonnaise

Mild salsa

Chopped fresh cilantro (optional)

1 Split the rolls in half and toast them.

2 Layer roast beef and a pepper on each sandwich.

3 Mix some mayonnaise with a little salsa and a little chopped cilantro.

4 Spread the mayonnaise mixture on the rolls and replace the tops.

IF YOU'RE SO
INCLINED

For a quick dessert, put 12 ounces of firm silken (custard-style) tofu in a food processor or blender container. Add $1/3$ cup, or to taste, of chocolate drink mix, and a splash of vanilla. Whirl until smooth, and serve. This makes 3 servings.

Use a serrated knife to cut tomatoes. It's less likely to slip, and it makes it easier to control how thin the slices are. Older kids can cut their own tomatoes with a steak knife.

Do-Your-Own Wraps

Deli wraps, which also go by names such as Rollups and WrapUps, are basically extra-thin, extra-large tortillas. Let the kids make their own sandwiches. Rollups are large, and half of one makes a kid-size sandwich.

Leaf lettuce

Tomatoes

Wraps (or extra-large tortillas)

Light mayonnaise or reduced-fat cream cheese

Thinly sliced deli meats: turkey breast, roast beef, lean ham

1 Wash the leaf lettuce and shake it dry.

2 Thinly slice the tomatoes.

3 Lightly spread each wrap with mayonnaise or cream cheese.

4 Lay the meat over the wrap in a thin layer.

5 Top the meat with 2 or 3 slices of tomato, then a lettuce leaf.

6 Roll up the bread and fillings tightly. Cut in half, and serve.

Peanut Butter and Jelly Stacks

I once was making peanut butter and jelly sandwiches, and realized I had only three slices of bread left. So I stacked them, then cut the sandwich in half and gave each kid two quarters. Now, of course, Lian and Daniel request these "triple" sandwiches.

Thin sandwich bread (whole wheat, white, or a combo)
Peanut butter
Jam or jelly of your choice

1 For each sandwich, place 3 slices on bread on a clean surface.

2 Spread 2 of the slices with peanut butter and jelly.

3 Stack them atop each other, with the peanut butter and jelly facing up.

4 Top with the remaining slice.

5 Cut each sandwich diagonally into quarters.

QUICK 𝗻 PAINLESS

If your child won't eat the "heel" of the bread (the end of the loaf), just make the sandwich so the crust is inside, rather than facing out. Bet she never notices.

A COMPLETE WASTE OF TIME

The 3 Worst Things to Do with Deli Foods:

1. Let them sit in a hot car.

2. Let them stand out on the picnic table while your kids' team plays an entire baseball game, start to finish.

3. Blame the mayonnaise if you ignore No. 1 and No. 2 and get sick. If anything, the vinegar in it helps keep "bugs" at bay.

Tuna and Cukes in Pockets

Water-packed tuna

Pita pocket breads

Sliced cucumber, or drained cucumber salad

Plain nonfat yogurt or sour cream

Fresh or dried dillweed (optional)

1 Drain the tuna.

2 Cut the pita breads in half and gently pull open to make pockets.

3 Warm the pita breads in a microwave (don't overheat) or toaster oven.

4 Fill each pita pocket with tuna and cucumber slices. Top with a dab of yogurt or sour cream, and sprinkle with a bit of dill, if desired.

Baked Bean Sandwiches

These are a long-standing tradition in New England. They're good cold, but if that doesn't appeal to you, you can always reheat the beans a bit.

Buns (rye, whole wheat, or white)

Butter or margarine

Baked beans (from a can or the deli)

1   Toast the buns. Spread with just a little butter or margarine.

2   Mash the beans with a fork.

3   Spread the beans on the bottom buns.

4   Replace the top buns.

5   Serve with carrot and celery sticks, and/or cut-up apples.

QUICK ⬥ PAINLESS

Some canned baked beans can be awfully sweet. If you like them with a touch more bite, just stir in a teaspoon of cider vinegar.

Carrot Sandwich Hearts

Thin sandwich bread

Shredded carrot salad

Reduced-fat cream cheese, or peanut butter

1 Cut the bread into heart shapes using a small sharp paring knife, or a large heart-shaped cookie cutter.

2 Mix the carrot salad 50-50 with cream cheese or peanut butter.

3 Carefully spread the mixture on half of the bread hearts. Top with the remaining bread hearts.

Getting Time on Your Side

	The Old Way	The Lazy Way
Making dinner before you rush off to the PTA	30 minutes	2 minutes
Cooking shrimp	3 minutes	Already cooked
Roasting chicken	2 hours	Already roasted
Making sandwich "wraps"	15 minutes	Let the kids do it
Waiting for chocolate pudding to set	45 minutes	No need to
Making potato salad	35 minutes	Just buy it

No Mess, No Fuss

My husband longs for the day when he'll be able to walk into the kitchen without sticking to the floors. I tell him that, short of completely mopping the floor every day (yeah, right), he'll just have to wait until the kids are in college.

The good news is that floors "clean enough to eat off" really aren't necessary. Nobody but the dog and the cat eat off of them. Well, maybe your 9-month-old son, too, but he needs to build up his immunity anyway (just kidding!).

That does not mean cleanliness is not important in the kitchen. It's very important, especially when you have kids.

KEEP IT CLEAN, KEEP IT SAFE

Let's start at the top: food safety and kitchen hygiene. A food-borne illness that would make you groan for a few days could seriously sicken, or kill, your child. The rules of food safety can be boiled down to these:

Keep hot foods hot and cold foods cold. Bacteria grow rapidly between the temperatures of 40°F and 140°F. Refrigerate both cooked and uncooked foods promptly.

To kill germs on kitchen sponges, put them in the top rack of the dishwasher when you run a load. Or zap them in the microwave for 1 minute (do this only with natural or cellulose sponges, not metal or rubberized scrubbers).

Treat raw meats, poultry, fish, and eggs as though they're automatically contaminated with bacteria. When you've handled any of these foods raw, wash your hands and everything that the food—and your hands—may have touched with hot, soapy water.

Cook meats, poultry, fish, and eggs all the way through. That means the yolk and white are set, the juices run clear, there's no longer any pink in the middle. Alas, that also means you really shouldn't feed your kids cookie dough that has raw egg in it. The risk is very small, but not worth taking.

Remember those often-overlooked sources of germs: sponges and towels. Buy antibacterial kitchen sponges and clean them often, and change the towels every day. Use one towel for wiping off dishes and another for drying hands.

Wash produce. Many harmful bacteria live on the surface of foods, so rinse all fresh produce thoroughly. On the other hand, some food safety experts recommend not washing meats and poultry, since splashing water can actually spread any bacteria to your sink and counters. If you do rinse meats, clean up carefully afterward.

Keep cutting boards and counters clean and dry. Plastic or glass boards can be run through the dishwasher. Any kind should be thoroughly washed with hot and soapy water after every use, and either air-dried (prop it up so air can circulate) or patted dry with a paper towel (not the kitchen towel, which may have germs). Occasionally, flood the board with a solution of 2 teaspoons liquid bleach in 1 quart of water; let it stand for a couple of minutes, then rinse thoroughly.

- Keep counters clean and dry. After every meal, wipe down the counters and kitchen table with a soapy sponge or an antibacterial spray. Rinse, and wipe down so they dry quickly. (Like us, bacteria need moisture, and thrive in wet environments.)

- Wash your hands a lot when you're preparing food, and insist that your kids wash their hands before setting the table, eating, or preparing food.

- Don't eat in any restaurant where the insects out-number you.

ORGANIZE TO SAVE STEPS

A friend who runs a cleaning business said she's amazed at how many people don't have their kitchens organized in any sort of logical order. The plates are in one place, the bowls across the kitchen in another cabinet—and neither is close to the dishwasher or table. This requires a lot of unnecessary steps, and makes it much harder to keep the kitchen tidy.

How you zone your kitchen depends, of course, on whether it's the size of a castle or a closet, and whether you have counters and cupboards to infinity or have to look through a microscope to find them. But, as a rule of thumb, here's the best way to organize. It's based on the tried-but-true triangle of stove, sink, and refrigerator.

IF YOU'RE SO INCLINED

Rather than just one cutting board, you might want to get three, to segregate germs and odors: a small one just for garlic and onions; a larger one reserved for raw meats, poultry, and fish; and another large one for vegetables and other foods.

QUICK **n** PAINLESS

If your kids often forget to wash their hands before eating dinner or setting the table, keep a bottle of colorful waterless hand soap on the kitchen table where they can't miss it. Don't overuse these alcohol-based gels, though; they're very drying to the skin.

Cooking/Food Preparation Area

This is where the stovetop, oven, and microwave are—in other words, where you will be preparing and cooking meals. Here is what you'll need:

- Pots and pans
- Cutting board(s)
- Spices
- Cooking oils
- Salt and pepper
- Serving bowls and platters
- Measuring cups and spoons
- Knives—make sure they're out of kids' reach!
- Cooking and food preparation utensils (vegetable peeler, spatula, etc.)

Baking Area

Obviously, you need this only if you bake. It should be near the oven. Here, you should put:

- Mixer
- Measuring cups and spoons
- Mixing bowls and utensils
- Baking pans
- Flour, sugar, baking powder, baking soda
- Baking mixes
- Shortening
- Sweeteners such as honey, molasses, and corn syrup

Eating/Serving/Cleanup Area

This includes the sink and the dishwasher, which in turn should not be too far from the kitchen table. Here you want to keep:

- Glasses and cups
- Silverware
- Dinner and dessert plates
- Bowls
- Coffee mugs and coffeemaker
- Napkins
- Toothpicks
- Kitchen towels and paper towels
- Garbage container and bags

Food Storage Area

This is where the refrigerator and the pantry—if you're lucky enough to have one—are. If you don't have a pantry, the cabinets you store food in should be nearby. That way when you come in from grocery shopping, you and the kids can dump all the bags in one corner of the kitchen and put food away without running all over the place. This is where you keep:

- Canned and dry goods such as soups and pasta
- Refrigerated and frozen foods
- Grocery lists and coupons
- Scissors
- Foil, plastic wrap, waxed paper, food storage bags

YOU'LL THANK YOURSELF LATER

Store all the "stickies"—molasses, corn syrup, vanilla extract,—in one cupboard, on a shelf lined with shelf paper. When it's cupboard cleaning time, just throw the sticky shelf paper away and replace it

SQUEAKY CLEAN

The number one way to cut down on your housecleaning effort is to enlist your spouse and kids. One charming thing about young children is that they actually like to do housework. They can't wait to get their hands on a broom or mop. Unfortunately, they quickly outgrow this stage, at which point you move into Stage Two: bribery and/or threats. Many child development "experts" don't recommend bribery or threats, but that's OK—let them have the dirty kitchens.

This isn't a general housecleaning book, so I'll confine myself to the most common cleaning headaches you inadvertently agree to when you decide, "Hey, wouldn't it be nice to have kids?"

Cut Elbow Grease with These Supplies

You can buy a whole closet full of fancy commercial cleaners, but you don't really need most of them. What you do need are these items, which may already be sitting in your kitchen, laundry room, or bathroom:

- Distilled vinegar
- Commercial "degummer" (such as Di-Solv-It or Goo Gone)
- Bleach (or another disinfectant)
- Rubbing alcohol and/or hairspray
- Eraser (the standard pink school kind is fine)
- Cornstarch
- Club soda

IF YOU'RE SO INCLINED

The ideal time to give the refrigerator a major-league cleaning is when you're going on a vacation or have just returned from one. When else (besides when you move) is it going to be so empty of food?

- Enzyme prewash stain remover (the ones that come in spray bottles

- Baking soda and/or borax

- Fels Naptha soap (optional)

As you'll see, these "low-tech" products can be used to clean both the kitchen and your kids' clothes.

A Sparkling Kitchen in a Jiffy

- All-purpose cleaning. For mopping floors and wiping down cabinets and counters, use a solution of ¼ cup vinegar to 1 gallon warm water. It's strong enough to cut grease, dirt, and sticky residues without leaving behind a vinegar odor. Note: If you've previously waxed the floor, this will peel it.

- Stains on laminate counters. Fruit juice plus kids equals purple counters. Use bleach or any cleaner that contains it. You also can use a paste of dishwasher detergent (which contains bleach) and water. Dab or spray the stain, let sit for a minute, then rinse.

- Gummy stuff. That is, the residue that results when your son decorates your cabinets with his stickers, your daughter decides the underside of the chair is a good place to park chewed gum, or you finally discover that ancient smashed raisin in the corner. Use a commercial degummer; it will work much better than freezing, peanut butter, or whatever else you've read about.

QUICK 🔲 *PAINLESS*

Keeping the kitchen clean is easiest if you break the job into segments. One day, clean the counters and small appliances. The next day, wipe down the cabinets. The third day, mop the floor. And so on.

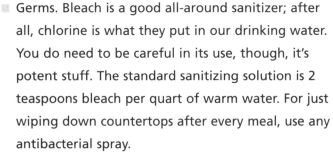

■ Germs. Bleach is a good all-around sanitizer; after all, chlorine is what they put in our drinking water. You do need to be careful in its use, though, it's potent stuff. The standard sanitizing solution is 2 teaspoons bleach per quart of warm water. For just wiping down countertops after every meal, use any antibacterial spray.

■ Food smells. After two months, you finally found your son's thermos—under his bed, with traces of furry chicken noodle soup still clinging to it. (And you thought that smell was his socks.) Fill it with a solution of 4 tablespoons baking soda to a quart of water and let stand overnight, then rinse. Or use a borax solution; follow the package directions.

■ Pencil marks on walls and counters. This one's easy— use an eraser.

■ Ink on walls or counters. Use rubbing alcohol or hairspray, which works because it contains alcohol. (This works on clothing as well.)

■ Scuff marks. Try the eraser trick. If that doesn't work, use the commercial degummer.

Take the Pain Out of Stains

Children may not always eat their dinner, but they happily wear it. Here's how I combat clothing stains:

■ Grease or oil. While it's still fresh, you can spray it with the prewash stain remover. However, plain old cornstarch is one of the best grease fighters I've found. Sprinkle it on the grease spot, rub it in, and

YOU'LL THANK YOURSELF LATER

One friend of ours has bowed to reality and always keeps a mop and bucket of water near the kitchen. Whenever someone spills something, the mop is handy. (Note: Don't keep a bucket of water around if you have an infant or toddler; they can drown.)

let it sit overnight. Shake or scrape off the excess, and wash the clothing. I've used this to remove even old, set-in grease stains.

- Chocolate. Any parent can tell you this is the absolute worst. I've found that wetting the stain, then scrubbing with Fels Naptha soap, helps. Or spray with a stain remover, then soak overnight in a borax solution or soapy water.

- Multiple stains. Spray the worst areas with a pre-wash stain remover. Then soak overnight in a borax solution (follow the label directions) or in water to which you've added laundry soap.

- Berries, juice. Treat immediately. If a prewash stain remover doesn't lighten the stain, try this: Stretch the fabric over a bowl, then pour club soda through the stain. If you don't have club soda, carefully pour boiling water through the stain from a height of about two feet.

- Egg. Scrape it off, spray with a stain remover, soak in cold water, then launder.

- Vomit, spit-up, sour milk. Soak for at least an hour in a baking soda or borax solution, then launder.

Finally got the kitchen gleaming (well, OK, pretty clean)? It's time to clean yourself. Treat yourself to a long, hot bath or steamy shower and your favorite bath gel or aftershave.

The Lazy Way

Getting Time on Your Side

	The Old Way	The Lazy Way
Sanitizing kitchen sponge	2 minutes	0 to 1 minute
Finding the measuring cups	Maybe never	30 seconds
Putting away dishes	15 minutes	5 minutes
Getting kids to wash hands	5 minutes	30 seconds
Mopping up spills	5 minutes	1 minute
Cleaning sticky cupboards	5 minutes	30 seconds

Part 3

Get Ready, Get Set...

Are You Too Lazy to Read Get Ready, Get Set...

1   It's a mystery how your 4-year-old son manages to keep growing. As far as you can tell, the kid's been living on bread and air for the past six months. ☐ yes ☐ no

2   You still have nightmares about your high school algebra teacher, and quake at the thought of trying to figure out whether your family's getting less than 30 percent of its calories from fat. ☐ yes ☐ no

3   Your son thinks fruits and vegetables are part of an alien plot to wipe out life on earth. ☐ yes ☐ no

six

Crash Course in Nutrition

Here's something that may surprise you: When it comes to eating, kids often know best. A few years back, some researchers put kids' eating to the test. They set out all kinds of foods, from broccoli to brownies, and let the children freely help themselves. They found that, while the kids varied a lot in their choices and the amount of food they ate from meal to meal, over the course of several days most of them ate a well-balanced diet.

The key is that the researchers gave the kids access to a variety of foods. As long as you do the same, your children should thrive. After all, if your 4-year-old is growing steadily, he isn't really living on air.

Plus you don't have to dredge up dim memories of high school algebra to figure out if your kids are eating well. Here's the short list of what to focus on to make sure your family is on the right path, nutritionally speaking.

A COMPLETE WASTE OF TIME

The 3 Worst Things to Do with an Overweight Child:

1. Put him on a diet.

2. Single her out from the rest of the family.

3. Encourage couch-potato habits.

BODY LANGUAGE

Kids come in all shapes and sizes, and it's important to make them feel comfortable with themselves and their bodies. But if your children are putting on weight and you know it's because they (and you) spend too much time in the fast-food joints and on the couch, or if your family has cut way back on fat and your kids' growth seems to be slowing down a lot, it's time to take a good look at your whole family's eating and exercise habits.

As for the child who seems too big or too small for her age, pediatricians say that in most cases, there's nothing to worry about. What's most important is your individual child's growth, not how he stacks up alongside his classmates.

Kids also grow in spurts, and may seem pudgy one month (or year) and beanpole-thin the next. This is perfectly normal for most kids.

Don't forget that kids need to pack a lot of calories into a small package. Restricting calories or fat can rob rapidly growing children of nutrients and set them up for eating disorders. It's better, say experts, to emphasize physical activity and to eat more healthfully as a family, and let your child grow "into" her weight.

ACTIVITY

How much TV do your children watch? Are they spending hours playing video games or cruising the 'Net? Nutrition experts are concluding that staying active may be even more important than what you eat. That holds true whether you're 4 or 74. In fact, many experts believe that kids today aren't really eating more calories than they did a couple of decades ago—but they are moving less. No wonder one in four kids is overweight.

Maybe like so many parents, you must leave your older child alone or with a neighbor for an hour or two a day, until you get home from work. Or maybe your neighborhood parks aren't as safe as you would like them to be, so letting your kids play there alone is out of the question.

The laziest alternative, assuming safe transportation is available, is to book your kids into after-school classes or teams that encourage physical activity. Dance, gymnastics, martial arts, baseball, swimming, basketball, and soccer are just some of the possibilities.

If outside activities aren't possible, try to come up with fun things the kids can do without leaving the house. Put up a basketball hoop. Buy some weights. Encourage your kids to jump rope to their favorite CDs.

Better yet, try exercising as a family, maybe by walking, riding bikes, or skating after dinner. After all, exercise is just as important for you as it is for your kids.

VARIETY

Kids routinely go through phases where they'll eat only white foods, or orange foods, or for that matter, just one food. But whether they eat it or not, your kids (and you) should have access to a bunch of foods in different colors: red, yellow, orange, green, white, and brown. I'm talking natural colors here, not neon blue and blinding orange.

QUICK 🔲 PAINLESS

Put on a lively CD, don some old clothes, and dance around the living room with your kids. It's fun, it requires no special talents or equipment, and it's a great way to act silly and get in some quality time with the kids—not to mention some exercise for all of you.

QUICK **n** PAINLESS

Most adults and kids over the age of 5 should eat only about 3 ounces of meat (or poultry, or fish) a day. But what's 3 ounces of meat? Think of a deck of cards—that's about how large the serving should be.

Brown is a tricky color. Basically, follow this rule of thumb:

- If it's brown, starchy, and low in fat—brown rice, whole wheat bread, pretzels—serve all you want.

- If it's brown and used to cluck, moo, oink, or bleat, serve it in moderation: one serving a day, or less.

- If it's brown, spreads on bread, and goes with grape jelly, let the kids enjoy it in moderation; peanut butter is high in fat, but a good protein source and meat substitute.

GREASE

Who cares about fat? Kids can eat anything, right?

Not necessarily. Doctors report that even in the teen years, many Americans already show the early signs of future heart disease.

On the other hand, you have to be careful about restricting fat intake in kids. The American Academy of Pediatrics warns that you should *never* put infants and toddlers under the age of 2 on a fat-restricted diet of any sort. They and their brains are growing and developing very rapidly, and they need the fat. It's no accident that breast milk gets nearly half its calories from fat.

Kids from the age of 2 up to about the age of 5, children should gradually adopt a diet that contains no more than 30 percent of calories from fat. In other words, take it easy on the butter and oil, start replacing whole dairy products with reduced-fat or nonfat versions, serve leaner protein foods such as lean meats, beans, and poultry without the skin, and encourage your kids to eat more grains and cereals, fruits, and vegetables.

WHERE KIDS GET CALCIUM

Quick—which has more calcium, a handful of almonds or $1/2$ cup of cottage cheese? Bet the answer will surprise you.

Here are some foods that supply calcium, a mineral that growing kids need plenty of.

The National Academy of Sciences recommends that kids 1 to 3 get 500 mg of calcium a day; kids 4 to 8, 800 mg; and kids 9 to 18, 1,300 mg. (Infants should be breast-fed or fed formula, so calcium is not a concern.)

Yogurt, plain, low-fat or nonfat (8 oz.)	415 mg
Yogurt, fruit (8 oz.)	345 mg
Milk (1 cup)	300 mg
Calcium-enriched orange juice (1 cup)	300 mg
Calcium-enriched soy or rice drink (1 cup)	300 mg
Hard cheese, such as Swiss or Cheddar	175 to
($1^1/2$ oz., or $1/3$ cup diced)	275 mg
Canned salmon, with bones, drained	180 mg
($1/2$ cup)	
Canned sardines, with bones (4)	180 mg
Parmesan cheese, grated (2 tbsp.)	175 mg
Dark molasses, 1 tbsp.*	100 mg
Frozen yogurt, low-fat or nonfat ($1/2$ cup)	150 mg
(small cone)	130 mg
Pudding, made from instant mix ($1/2$ cup)	150 mg
Tofu, made with calcium sulfate (1 oz.)	150 mg

YOU'LL THANK YOURSELF LATER

If your child insists on juice or soda after she's been playing hard on a hot day, water it down, either with water or plenty of ice. Too much sugar will slow down the rate at which her body absorbs the liquid.

QUICK n' PAINLESS

Not all high-fat foods are obvious. Use the "greasy napkin" test. If that blueberry muffin leaves a bunch of oily spots on your napkin, it's high in fat, regardless of the insistence of the guy behind the counter that it's not.

Cheese pizza, thin crust ($^1/_8$ of 12" pizza)	100 to 125 mg
Perch (baked, 3 oz.)	100 mg
Ice cream, vanilla, regular or low-fat ($^1/_2$ cup)	85 to 90 mg
Almonds, dry-roasted ($^1/_4$ cup)	90 mg
Waffle, whole-grain frozen (1)	84 mg
Bok choy, cooked ($^1/_2$ cup)	80 mg
Greens, turnip and beet ($^1/_2$ cup)	75 mg
Cottage cheese, lowfat ($^1/_2$ cup)	70 mg
Navy or Great Northern beans, canned ($^1/_2$ cup) (includes baked beans)	60 to 80mg
Light molasses (1 tbsp.)	60 mg
Shelf-stable pudding snacks ($3^1/_2$ oz.)	50 to 60 mg
Macaroni and cheese (prepared from box)	50 mg
Cooked kale	50 mg
Some breakfast cereals (before adding milk)	40 to 80 mg

*Blackstrap molasses has 170 mg of calcium per tablespoon, but is too bitter to appeal to most adults, let alone kids. You can hide a tablespoon or two in your gingerbread, though.

Source: USDA Nutrient Database for Standard Reference

WHERE KIDS GET IRON

Meats contain a kind of iron that's more easily absorbed by the body than the iron found in plant foods. Eating vegetable foods alongside meats or a food or drink rich in vitamin C helps the body better absorb the iron.

The National Academy of Sciences recommends that kids ages 6 months to 10 years get 10 mg of iron a day; boys 11 to 18, 12 mg; and girls 11 to 18, 15 mg. (Infants should be breast-fed or fed formula.)

Beef, sirloin (3 oz. cooked)	2.8 mg
Fortified breakfast cereals	2 to 8 mg
Lamb, sirloin (3 oz. cooked)	1.9 mg
Beans, white (navy, great northern, etc.), canned ($^1/_2$ cup)	2 to 3 mg
Beans, kidney or pinto (including refried), canned ($^1/_2$ cup)	1.6 to 1.8 mg
Soybeans, roasted (1 oz., or 3 tbsp.)	1.3 mg
Almonds, roasted ($^1/_4$ cup)	1.3 mg
Pork, tenderloin (3 oz. cooked)	1.2 mg
Dried prunes, figs, or apricots ($^1/_4$ cup)	1 to 1.5 mg
Pasta, enriched, cooked ($^1/_2$ cup)	1 mg
Rice, enriched, cooked ($^1/_2$ cup)	0.9 mg
Chicken, drumstick or thigh	0.7 to 0.8 mg

Source: USDA Nutrient Database for Standard Reference

BALANCE

One of my personal pet peeves is kids' menus in restaurants, which offer the same four monotonous, high-fat, high-salt meals: hot dog and fries, hamburger and fries, grilled cheese and fries, chicken strips and fries. You'd think they've never met a kid who eats salads and fruit.

"Balance" also means portion control. I cringe when I see a kid who can't be more than 10 eating a large double cheeseburger, giant fries, and a 32-ounce soft drink in a single sitting. That all-too-typical fast-food meal supplies nearly all the calories, and more than 100 percent of the fat and saturated fat, that a 10-year-old boy should eat in an entire day.

IF YOU'RE SO INCLINED

One way to teach toddlers portion control is to visually divide up foods. Take an old ice cube tray or small margarine containers, and put, say, three pretzels or four strawberries or six small crackers in each compartment. You can even turn it into a counting game.

On the other hand, completely shunning "bad" foods doesn't work. You don't have to keep cookies in the house, but forbidding your kid from ever having a cookie will just make them more desirable and encourage him to sneak them at a friend's house.

Like Grandma said: Moderation in all things.

CALCIUM AND IRON

Like adults, kids need a whole array of vitamins and minerals. But in proportion to body weight, kids have bigger requirements for calories, protein, calcium, and iron. Since the average American kid gets enough calories and protein, let's talk about calcium and iron.

Up to about the age of 25, kids add to bone density. Once we're adults, our bodies quit making new bone, and as we get older, we actually start losing bone (although exercise can help slow the loss). That's why it's so important that kids build up bone density while they're young—dem bones will have to carry them through many years of living.

Unfortunately, for a lot of kids, juice and soft drinks have replaced milk. This may be especially unfortunate for teen girls, who need a lot of calcium, about 1,200 mg a day. While you don't have to drink milk to get calcium, it's the easiest way to do it; one glass of milk (any kind) averages about 300 mg of the mineral. Milk also is fortified with vitamin D, which helps kids absorb calcium.

Iron deficiency anemia is one of the most common nutritional problems among American children, especially infants and toddlers, and teenage girls. Breast milk and

YOU'LL THANK YOURSELF LATER

If your kid won't touch plain milk, and your supermarket doesn't carry low-fat flavored milks, try this. Buy quarts of nonfat or low-fat milk and stir a different flavor of milk powder into each quart: strawberry, chocolate, or malt. Use only half to two-thirds the amount called for on the label (keeping in mind that there are 4 cups to a quart) to keep the sugar content down.

formula supply iron, but at about 6 months, infants need to start on solid food as well. Iron-fortified cereals are ideal. Never give your child iron supplements without a doctor's OK. Too much iron can be poisonous, which is why iron pills carry a safety warning.

Ironically, calcium can hinder iron absorption, so while you emphasize dairy foods for their calcium, you need to make sure your kids get plenty of iron-rich foods as well.

SWEETNESS

Despite what you may have heard, there is no proven link between sugar and hyperactivity. If anything, research has shown the opposite: Carbohydrates soothe.

But while sugar is no villain and does have its uses—what's a bowl of oatmeal without a spoonful of sugar?—it represents empty calories. One of the biggest offenders in this area: soft drinks. If soft drinks have replaced fruit juice, milk, and water for your family, you may be robbing your kids of essential nutrients such as calcium, vitamin C, and fluoride. Young children who drink more than a can of pop a day may also be getting too much caffeine. And you thought it was the sugar that had them bouncing off the walls!

Natural sugar isn't the cure, either. Pediatricians report that young children often drink way too much juice, and some recommend no more than 8 ounces (that's a cup) a day for a young child and 12 ounces (1$\frac{1}{2}$ cups) for school-agers. While it's better than soft drinks—at least it has nutrients—juice is high in sugar, and can give children diarrhea and fill them up so they don't eat enough.

QUICK ⦿ PAINLESS

An easy way to "hedge your bets" is to give your kids a multivitamin and mineral supplement, plus calcium tablets. Check with your pediatrician before giving your children supplements, and don't forget that they may already be getting a "multi-vitamin" in their fortified breakfast cereal.

QUICK ☜ⁿ⸱➤ PAINLESS

Here's How to Decipher
Juice Labels at a Glance:

1. "Juice" alone: It's
   made only from fruit
   or vegetable juice(s).

2. "Cocktail" or "drink":
   It has sugar and water
   in it.

3. "Flavored": It may be
   all juice (or not), but
   contains only a small
   amount of the flavor-
   ing juice listed.

Doctors caution that babies under the age of 6 months should not drink juice, only breast milk or formula.

WATER

I have to admit that, like most parents, my husband and I haven't quite figured out how to get our kids to drink enough water, short of hooking them up to an IV. Water is important to everybody, of course, but can be even more so to kids, since they don't tolerate extremes in heat as well as adults do. Toss in some vigorous playing in the backyard or in the park, and a kid can easily reach heat exhaustion. Water's important in the winter, too, when indoor heating dries out children's sensitive skin and noses.

Two things that can help:

- Water bottles. My children have big water bottles, little water bottles, water bottles that fit on their bikes, water bottles shaped like bunnies, and water bottles decorated with cartoon heroes. Before bedtime, I fill their water bottle and keep it at the head of the bed. Somehow, water tastes better when it's drunk from a Batman bottle.

- Bottled water, especially the fizzy or flavored kind. Waters that come in bottles, bubble, and taste like raspberry or orange have more pizzazz than the stuff from the tap. Make sure the water's unsweetened, of course. Do note that most bottled waters, unlike tap water, do not contain fluoride and thus will not protect kids' teeth.

TASTE

This is one of those things children understand so much better than adults. What good is good-for-you-food if it tastes lousy? You can force a child who doesn't like green beans to eat them, but only under pain of death or equally dire consequences, like taking away the Nintendo.

On the other hand, children also relish a good apple or strawberry. The average little kid doesn't think of strawberries as good for you and brownies as sinful. He just thinks both of them are yummy.

In other words, don't make your kid "earn" dessert by eating vegetables he hates. The only message you're sending him is that vegetables suck and dessert is awesome.

SET AN EXAMPLE

What do you eat? If you've never met a piece of chicken that wasn't fried and you shun milk for cola, how will you tell your kids they should eat peas and broiled chicken?

Likewise, if you gobble food, skip meals, or eat in front of the television, your children will no doubt do the same.

A COMPLETE WASTE OF TIME

The 3 Worst Things to Do with Dinner:

1. Spend it in front of the TV.

2. Eat it in the car.

3. Skip it.

Getting Time on Your Side

	The Old Way	The Lazy Way
Nagging about your kids' weight	Constant	Not to worry
Getting your kid to drink milk (includes time spent threatening)	Forget it	30 seconds
Figuring out whether the blueberry muffin is high in fat	10 minutes	10 seconds
Getting your kid to finish his peas so he can have pie	Hours	Don't bother
Exercising (old way includes drive to health club)	1 hour	30 minutes
Arguing "do as I say, not as I do"	Days	Not a problem

seven

Right Bites—Foods that Make the Grade

By now, you're probably saying to yourself, "All this is great—but what, exactly, should I feed my kids?"

The answer depends on you, your children, how old they are, and what you all like to eat. (As my son would say, "Duh.") But there are some foods that excel nutritionally. If your daughter announces that she's running off to live on a desert island, these are the first items you should pack.

I've called these top-scoring foods the "A" team. They provide generous doses of key nutrients (based on recommendations for kids ages 7 to 10).

Next to each food, I've listed all of the vitamins and minerals it's richest in. For what the different vitamins and minerals are and why they're important, see "If You Don't Know What It Means, Look Here."

To keep things simple, I've based servings on the Food Pyramid (see the next page). Keep in mind that those servings are fairly small, and that in some cases, I'm comparing, um, apples and oranges. Obviously, one banana is denser than $\frac{1}{2}$

The following symbols indicate fats, oils, and sugars naturally occuring and added.

Fats & Oils ———— ○
Sugars ———— ▼

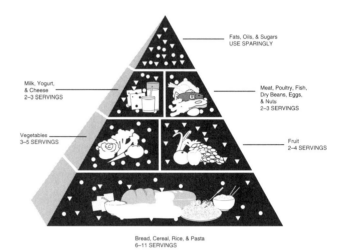

Fats, Oils, & Sugars
USE SPARINGLY

Milk, Yogurt,
& Cheese
2–3 SERVINGS

Meat, Poultry, Fish,
Dry Beans, Eggs,
& Nuts
2–3 SERVINGS

Vegetables
3–5 SERVINGS

Fruit
2–4 SERVINGS

Bread, Cereal, Rice, & Pasta
6–11 SERVINGS

USDA Food Pyramid. Source: U.S. Department of Agriculture

A COMPLETE WASTE OF TIME

The 3 Worst Things to Do with Fresh Vegetables:

1. Eat too few of them.

2. Overcook them (except in soup).

3. Leave them in the crisper drawer too long.

cup honeydew, and most kids would eat more melon than that. And ½ cup cooked spinach has more nutrients than 1 cup raw because it's a lot more spinach (before it's cooked down), plain and simple.

The Food Guide Pyramid can help you picture how many servings of various foods to feed your children. Younger children would eat the lowest number of servings; teenagers, the highest.

JUST WHAT IS A SERVING, ANYWAY?

Here's how the U.S. Department of Agriculture defines servings in its Food Guide Pyramid.

Bread, cereal, rice, pasta: 1 slice bread; 1 ounce ready-to-eat cereal; $1/2$ cup cooked cereal; $1/2$ cup cooked rice or pasta; 5 or 6 small crackers.

Vegetables: 1 cup raw, leafy greens; $1/2$ cup cooked or chopped raw vegetables; $3/4$ cup vegetable juice.

Fruit: 1 medium apple, banana, or orange; $1/2$ cup chopped, cooked, or canned fruit; $1/4$ cup dried fruit; $3/4$ cup fruit juice.

Milk, yogurt, and cheese: 1 cup milk or yogurt; $1 1/2$ ounces natural cheese; 2 ounces processed cheese.

Meat, poultry, fish, dry beans, eggs, and nuts: 2 to 3 ounces cooked lean meat, poultry, or fish. Foods that count as 1 ounce meat: $1/2$ cup cooked dry beans; 1 egg; 2 tablespoons peanut butter; $1/3$ cup nuts.

Fats, oils, and sweets: No serving recommendation, except to use sparingly.

(Note that, as a rough guideline, a serving for a child age 1 to 3 is 1 tablespoon of food per year of age. At the time of this writing, the U.S. government was in the process of setting standard serving sizes for children.)

I haven't obsessed over fat, sodium, and sugar. After all, some foods that are high in fat (such as cheese) or sodium (such as canned beans) have virtues that, as far as I'm concerned, outweigh their "vices." On the other hand, lean meats and low-fat dairy products are just as good, if not better, nutritionally than their fatty versions.

I've stuck pretty much to what's available in the supermarket and what most families are likely to buy. If

QUICK 💊 *PAINLESS*

You may know that you can cut a kiwifruit in half and scoop out the flesh with a spoon. An even easier way to eat it is whole, skin and all, like a peach. That makes the fruit really portable; your kids can just grab it and go.

you shop the natural food store every week and feed your kids quinoa (a definite "A" grain), more power to you.

By the way, just because foods aren't on this list doesn't mean your kid should never eat them. Why be a kid, after all, if you can't occasionally wash down a bunch of potato chips with green slime punch? (Hey, potato chips have vitamin C.)

THE "A" TEAM

Grains and Cereals

Serving sizes: 1 slice bread or 1 tortilla; $\frac{1}{2}$ cup cooked cereal, rice, or pasta; 1 ounce ready-to-eat cereal; 5 or 6 small crackers.

- Whole wheat bread (protein, fiber, thiamin, folate, magnesium, manganese, selenium)

- Oatmeal, regular (fiber, protein, thiamin, magnesium, manganese, phosphorus, selenium)

- Oatmeal, instant (fortified) (protein, fiber, vitamin A, thiamin, riboflavin, niacin, vitamin B_6, iron, calcium, magnesium, manganese, phosphorus)

- Whole wheat pasta (protein, fiber, magnesium, manganese, selenium)

- Bulgur, tabbouleh (fiber, vitamin A, vitamin C, vitamin E, folate, iron, magnesium)

- Barley, pearled (fiber, niacin, folate, iron, magnesium, selenium)

- Spaghetti, regular, enriched (protein, fiber, iron, thiamin, selenium)

- Brown rice (thiamin, niacin, vitamin B_6, magnesium, manganese, selenium)

- Ready-to-eat breakfast cereals (nutrients depend on brand, but all are fortified with vitamins and minerals; whole grain ones supply fiber as well)

- Cereal-based snack mix (vitamin B_{12}, folate, iron, thiamin)

- Flour tortilla, whole wheat (protein, thiamin, magnesium, phosphorus)

- Flour tortilla, regular (thiamin, selenium, protein, iron, niacin, riboflavin)

- White bread, enriched (protein, thiamin, folate, selenium)

- Whole wheat crackers (manganese, magnesium, fiber, vitamin E, selenium)

- Pretzels (folate, manganese, iron, riboflavin, thiamin, niacin)

- Popcorn, low-fat microwave, 3 cups popped (magnesium, fiber)

- White rice, converted, enriched (thiamin, iron, selenium)

- Wild rice (protein, folate, magnesium, zinc)

- Couscous (protein, folate)

- Corn tortilla (magnesium, phosphorus)

IF YOU'RE SO INCLINED

For a great breakfast treat, spread whole wheat tortillas with just a smear of butter or margarine, sprinkle lightly with sugar and cinnamon, and pop in the toaster oven (or regular oven) at 400°F until they turn crisp.

Vegetables

Serving sizes: 1 cup raw leafy greens; $^1/_2$ cup chopped and/or cooked vegetable; $^3/_4$ cup juice. All vegetables are lightly cooked, unless otherwise noted.

- Sweet potato, fresh (vitamin A, vitamin C, folate, manganese, potassium, vitamin B_6, fiber, copper, magnesium, riboflavin)

- Carrots, raw or lightly steamed (vitamin A, vitamin K, vitamin C, potassium, vitamin B_6)

- Spinach, raw (vitamin K, folate, vitamin A, vitamin C, magnesium)

- Red bell peppers (vitamin C, vitamin A, vitamin K, folate, vitamin B_6)

- Spinach, lightly cooked (folate, vitamin A, magnesium, vitamin C, magnesium, manganese, vitamin E, potassium, iron, riboflavin, vitamin B_6)

- Broccoli, raw or lightly steamed (vitamin C, folate, vitamin K, vitamin A, potassium, fiber)

- Brussels sprouts (vitamin K, vitamin C, folate, selenium, fiber, potassium)

- Winter squash (vitamin A, folate, vitamin C, potassium, fiber)

- Vegetable juice, canned, low-sodium (vitamin C, folate, vitamin A, copper, potassium, vitamin B_6, magnesium)

- Kale (vitamin A, vitamin C, manganese)

- Asparagus (folate, vitamin K, vitamin C, thiamin, riboflavin)

IF YOU'RE SO INCLINED

Even fairly young kids can help prepare asparagus, if you don't mind some short stalks. Show them how to gently bend the bottom third of the stalk until the woody part snaps off.

- Green bell peppers (vitamin C, vitamin K, folate, vitamin B_6)
- Snow peas (vitamin C, folate, iron, manganese, fiber, thiamin)
- Avocado (vitamin K, folate, potassium, fiber, magnesium, vitamin B_6, vitamin E, niacin, vitamin B_6, vitamin E, vitamin C, copper)
- Artichoke hearts, frozen (folate, fiber, magnesium, potassium)
- Cauliflower (vitamin C, folate, vitamin K)
- Romaine lettuce (folate, vitamin C, vitamin A, manganese)
- Leaf lettuce (vitamin K, folate, vitamin C, manganese, vitamin A)
- Bok choy (vitamin C, folate, vitamin A, potassium, vitamin B_6, calcium)
- Green beans (vitamin K, folate, vitamin C, fiber)
- Green peas, frozen (folate, thiamin, fiber, vitamin C, protein, magnesium, iron, manganese)
- Potato, baked, medium, with skin (protein, fiber, thiamin, niacin, vitamin B_6, vitamin C, folate, vitamin K, pantothenic acid, copper, iron, magnesium, manganese, potassium)
- Collard greens, cooked (vitamin A, vitamin C, vitamin E, fiber)
- Corn, frozen (folate, fiber)
- Boston or Bibb lettuce (folate, vitamin C)

YOU'LL THANK YOURSELF LATER

If you're lucky enough to find fresh baby artichokes in your market, don't pass them up. You need only peel the outer leaves, then quickly steam or sauté the artichokes. The kids might find them more appealing if you explain they're flowers.

Although it may be tempting to eat them right away, supermarket tomatoes always need time to finish ripening. Let them stand out at room temperature for at least a day or two.

- Cabbage, raw (vitamin C, folate)
- Mushrooms, raw (selenium, riboflavin, copper, niacin)
- Tomato, raw (vitamin C, vitamin K, folate, potassium)
- Tomatoes, cooked (vitamin C, potassium, vitamin A)
- Frozen hash browns, cooked (niacin, vitamin C)
- Beets, canned (folate, iron)
- Iceberg lettuce (folate)
- Summer squash (folate, magnesium, vitamin C)
- Cucumber, raw (selenium)

Fruits

Serving sizes: 1 whole fruit (for fruits normally eaten that way), $\frac{1}{2}$ cup berries or chopped fruit, $\frac{1}{4}$ cup dried fruit, or $\frac{3}{4}$ cup juice.

- Citrus fruits: orange, tangelo, tangerine, grapefruit (vitamin C, folate, fiber)
- Kiwifruit, minus skin (vitamin C, fiber, magnesium, potassium, vitamin E)
- Cantaloupe (vitamin C, vitamin A, folate, potassium)
- Citrus juices: orange, grapefruit (vitamin C, folate, potassium)
- Papaya, fresh (vitamin C, folate, vitamin E)
- Mango, fresh (vitamin C, vitamin A, vitamin E, folate)
- Strawberries (vitamin C, vitamin K, folate)

- Banana (vitamin B_6, vitamin C, folate, potassium, magnesium, fiber, riboflavin)

- Pineapple, fresh (manganese, vitamin C)

- Apricots, fresh (vitamin A, vitamin C, potassium, vitamin E)

- Apricots, dried (vitamin A, potassium, iron)

- Raspberries (vitamin C, manganese, fiber, folate)

- Honeydew melon (vitamin C, potassium)

- Peaches, with skin (vitamin K, vitamin C, vitamin E, potassium, fiber)

- Cherimoya, or custard apple (vitamin C, fiber, thiamin, niacin, riboflavin)

- Star fruit, or carambola (vitamin C, fiber, folate)

- Blueberries (vitamin C, fiber, vitamin E)

- Pears, Bartlett (fiber, vitamin C, copper, vitamin E, folate, potassium)

- Nectarines (vitamin K, vitamin E, vitamin C, vitamin A, fiber, potassium, niacin)

- Prunes, or dried plums as they're calling them these days (vitamin B_6, fiber, potassium, copper, iron, magnesium)

- Apples, with skin (vitamin K, vitamin C, fiber)

- Grapes, green (selenium, vitamin C)

- Watermelon (vitamin C)

- Cherries, sweet (vitamin C)

- Plums (vitamin C)

QUICK ⬛ PAINLESS

Bet your kids don't know the easiest way yet to "brush" their teeth: Eat an apple and a slice of hard cheese, such as Cheddar. The apple cleans teeth, removing some plaque, and the cheese helps slow the formation of enamel-destroying acids.

QUICK ⟨ɪɪɪ⟩ PAINLESS

To keep it juicy, cook pork tenderloin quickly. Sprinkle some herbs on a ³/₄-pound tenderloin and roast it in a 450°F oven for 20 to 25 minutes, or until it reaches 160°F in the center. Let stand for 5 minutes, then slice.

Meats and Other Protein-Rich Foods

Serving sizes: 3 ounces cooked meat, fish, or poultry; ¹/₄ cup cooked beans or tofu; 1 ounce nuts or seeds.

- Beef, top sirloin (protein, zinc, iron, niacin, vitamin B_6, phosphorus, vitamin B_{12}, riboflavin, potassium, magnesium)

- Pork, tenderloin (selenium, protein, thiamin, vitamin B_{12}, vitamin B_{12}, niacin, phosphorus, vitamin B_6, iron)

- Dried beans (navy, kidney, pinto, etc.), peas, and lentils, cooked from scratch, frozen, or canned (folate, fiber, protein, magnesium, iron, potassium, phosphorus, thiamin, copper)

- Fish, salmon, fresh (vitamin B_{12}, protein, niacin, vitamin B_6, thiamin, folate, phosphorus, potassium, magnesium, vitamin E, riboflavin)

- Fish, perch (vitamin B_{12}, protein, manganese, phosphorus, magnesium, vitamin E, potassium, zinc, niacin, calcium, copper, iron)

- Tuna, water-packed, drained, ¹/₄ cup (selenium, vitamin B_{12}, protein, niacin, vitamin D)

- Chicken breast (protein, niacin, selenium, vitamin B_6, phosphorus, vitamin B_{12}, magnesium)

- Lamb, sirloin (vitamin B_{12}, protein, selenium, zinc, niacin, phosphorus, riboflavin, iron, folate, potassium, magnesium, thiamin, vitamin B_6)

- Sunflower seeds, 3 tablespoons, hulled (vitamin E, selenium, folate, phosphorus, copper, manganese, magnesium, protein, fiber, vitamin B_6, niacin, zinc)

- Almonds, ¼ cup (magnesium, copper, vitamin E, manganese, phosphorus, fiber, folate, protein, riboflavin, zinc, potassium, iron, calcium)

- Egg, whole (vitamin K, vitamin B_{12}, selenium, protein, folate, riboflavin, vitamin A, phosphorus, niacin)

- Peanut butter (vitamin E, magnesium, niacin, protein, folate, phosphorus, potassium)

- Tofu, firm, made with nigari (folate, selenium, manganese, protein, magnesium, phosphorus, calcium, copper, iron)

- Walnuts, ¼ cup (manganese, magnesium, copper, folate, protein, vitamin B_6, thiamin, vitamin E)

- Egg substitute (depends on the brand, but the popular brands have protein, iron, and some vitamin A)

- Egg white (selenium, protein, riboflavin)

Dairy Foods

Unless otherwise noted, servings are 1 cup.

- Yogurt, low-fat, plain or fruit (vitamin B_{12}, calcium, protein, riboflavin, phosphorus, potassium, folate, magnesium, zinc, selenium)

- Milk, regular, low-fat, or nonfat (vitamin B_{12}, calcium, riboflavin, vitamin K, protein, phosphorus, vitamin D, magnesium, selenium, potassium, folate)

- Cheeses (Cheddar, Swiss, American processed), ⅓ cup diced or 3 thin slices (calcium, protein, vitamin B_{12}, vitamin A, phosphorus, selenium, zinc)

You fed the kids a nutritious dinner and they're tucked away in bed. Curl up on the sofa and watch that favorite movie you've been meaning to get to.

The Lazy Way

Getting Time on Your Side

	The Old Way	The Lazy Way
Preparing a kiwifruit	30 seconds	0 seconds
Making sure the kids get enough vitamin C	You're never sure	No problem
Roasting pork	50 minutes	25 minutes
Preparing asparagus	10 minutes	Let the kids do it
Getting enough fiber	Hard to figure	No problem
Cleaning teeth	3 minutes	1 minute

Sustaining Supermarket Sanity

Here's how one mom describes her weekly trip to the supermarket:

"After one of my daughters landed on her head once, after reaching out of the cart to grab something that interested her, that was the last time I put a toddler in the back of a shopping cart. That leaves the baby in the front, and the toddler girls roaming free. They behave fairly well, considering their age, but I wish I had eyes in the back of my head, an extra pair of hands, or a nanny! We zip through the store on a mission to purchase what we need for the week in under an hour, before the baby starts crying for his next meal. Supermarkets aren't exactly a conducive environment for nursing.

"When we get to the checkout, I always hear the same thing: 'Miss, did you know this is opened? Miss, did you know this is opened?' By that time, I've bribed the girls to be quiet by opening half of the items in the cart."

IF YOU'RE SO
INCLINED

Use your computer to type up a list of items you buy frequently, and make a bunch of printouts. When it's time to shop, just cross out whatever you don't need. Be sure to leave room for scribbling notes and listing miscellaneous stuff.

Technically, of course, one is not supposed to open boxes before purchasing them. But then, one is also not supposed to bribe children to behave—ha! Do remember, you open it, you pay for it.

So how do you shop with kids? That's easy: You leave them home. Better yet, send them shopping with your spouse while you stay home. Unfortunately, life is not always so easy, especially if you lack a spouse (there are limits to what you can ask friends to do). Frankly, I have no stunning insights into shopping with kids, but have gleaned a few hints, from my own and other parents' experiences.

TRIED-AND-TRUE WAYS TO SPEED UP SHOPPING

Let's face it: When you go to the supermarket, especially with children, your mission is to get in and out of the place as quickly as possible. Here are some strategies that can help you do that.

Make a List, and Check It Twice

This is far and away the best strategy for saving both time and money. Wandering the aisles listlessly looking for this and that wastes time and makes it more likely that you'll buy things on impulse—and still not come home with what you actually need.

Make sure the shopping list is readily accessible to both you and your spouse, and to your kids, if they're older. The refrigerator door is a good place to post it. Also, make sure to jot down items as soon as you notice you're running low.

PRODUCE

Broccoli _____

Carrots_____ regular _____ baby

Red peppers _____

Bagged salad _____

Lettuce _____

Potatoes _____

Other veggies _____

_____

Herbs _____

Apples _____

Bananas _____

Other fruit _____

_____

CANNED/PACKED STUFF

Beans _____

Rice _____

Pasta _____

Macaroni and cheese _____

Tomatoes _____

Peanut butter _____

Jelly _____

Other _____

_____

SNACKS / DRINKS

Crackers _____

Fruit juices _____

Pop _____

Other _____

_____

FISH

Shrimp _____ raw _____ cooked

Salmon _____

Other fish _____

_____

DELI / BREAD / SALAD BAR

Tortillas _____

Sandwich bread _____

Pizza crust _____

Roast chicken _____

Salads _____

Other _____

_____

Sample Shopping List.

MEATS

Hamburger _____

Chicken breast _____

Cut-up chicken _____

Beef _____

Pork _____

Ground turkey _____

Turkey breast _____

Other _____

_____

DAIRY

Butter _____

1% milk _____

Yogurt _____

Cottage cheese _____

Cheese _____

Other _____

_____

FROZEN

Vegetables _____

Waffles _____

Ice cream _____

Sorbet _____

Juice/pop bars _____

Other _____

_____

_____

_____

PHARMACY

Toothpaste _____

Shampoo _____

Conditioner _____

Vitamins _____

Other _____

HOUSEHOLD

Dishwasher detergent _____

Dishwasher liquid _____

Soap _____

Paper towels _____

Napkins _____

Cleaners _____

Other _____

_____

YOU'LL THANK YOURSELF LATER

For easier shopping, break your standard shopping list into two lists: a weekly one, for perishables (meats, produce, and so on); and a monthly one, for packaged goods and frozen foods.

QUICK **n** PAINLESS

Want to cut to the chase on the food label? Look for:

1. Percent of calories from fat.

2. Whether there's something besides zeros next to the nutrients (A, C, calcium, iron).

3. The first ingredient listed. It's the most predominant, by weight.

To shop most efficiently, arrange the list by sections or aisles of the store.

Shop at the Same Market All the Time

No doubt you already do this, but it bears mentioning anyway. If you pick a favorite store and stick to it, you'll be able to memorize where everything is, and not waste time looking for the canned pineapple or the toothpicks.

Keep on Task

I never buy frozen dinners, so I simply skip that aisle. No doubt there are foods you never buy. Don't get distracted by sales for items you don't want; just cruise through without stopping.

By the same token, learn to "speed read" food labels. For a given product, zero in on what's most important to you. For hot dogs, it might be grams of fat; for juice, it might be vitamin C content.

Concentrate on the Perimeter of the Store

There are three reasons for this:

- **Nutrition.** Most of the less processed, freshest foods, such as produce, meats, fish, and deli and bakery items, usually are arranged around the outside of the store. Well, yes, the doughnuts and croissants are there, too, but you can ignore them.

- **Practicality.** Life won't grind to a halt if you forget to buy graham crackers (although forgetting the toilet paper could pose a problem), but forget the milk and bread, and you'll be scrambling.

Nutrition Facts

Serving Size 1/2 cup (114g)
Servings Per Container 4

Amount Per Serving

Calories 90   Calories from Fat 30

	% Daily Value*
Total Fat 3g	5%
Saturated Fat 0g	0%
Cholesterol 0mg	0%
Sodium 300mg	13%
Total Carbohydrate 13g	4%
Dietary Fiber 3g	12%
Sugars 3g	
Protein 3g	

Vitamin A 80%	•	Vitamin C 60%
Calcium 4%	•	Iron 4%

*Percent Daily Values are based on a 2,000 calorie diet. Your daily values may be higher or lower depending on your calorie needs:

	Calories:	2,000	2,500
Total Fat	Less than	65g	80g
Sat Fat	Less than	20g	25g
Cholesterol	Less than	300mg	300mg
Sodium	Less than	2,400mg	2,400mg
Total Carbohydrate		300g	375g
Dietary Fiber		25g	30g

Food label.

 Speed. The fewer aisles you travel down, the faster you can get out of the store.

Purchase Staples in Bulk

If you buy paper goods and packaged goods in larger quantities, preferably when you're shopping alone, you can skip those aisles on most of your trips to the store, and concentrate on the perishables.

SHOPPING SECRETS, BY AGE

Take an 18-month-old shopping, and it's a struggle just to keep him in the cart. Take an 11-year-old shopping, and you have a helper. Here are some strategies used by parents with children of various ages.

YOU'LL THANK YOURSELF LATER

Never buy just one or two things at the grocery store. If you need to go to the store for milk, make a quick mini-list of other items—enough to just make your express lane's cut-off.

A COMPLETE WASTE OF TIME

The 3 Worst Things to Do When Shopping with Toddlers or Preschoolers:

1. Take them down the candy aisle.

2. Give them more than two choices about any-thing.

3. Let them push the cart.

Little Kids (Ages 1 to 4)

For toddlers and preschoolers, your best hope is to get in and out of the store as quickly as possible. Other than that:

Feed Them

Give the kids a handful of raisins, a cracker, breast milk, whatever you have on hand—just before you take them to the store. They'll still clamor, but maybe not as loudly if they're not hungry.

Distract Them

I've always wondered why they put blinders on horses but not kids—they would come in so handy in the check-out lane. Until someone picks up this brilliant marketing idea, you'll basically have to rely on your own wiles. Try a board book, finger puppets, and anything else you can think of, especially when you're passing the cookies: "Hey look, isn't that Barney? No, over there, by the bread flour…"

Tell Them "No," and Mean It

Like so much of parenting, this is easier said than done. But grocery stores, with all their temptations, are prime places for prolonged tantrums and whining. Ever watch (or, worse, participate in) this scenario? Child asks for candy, dad says no, child cries, dad says no again, child throws a fit, dad says, "OK, OK, be quiet already, you can have the candy." Moral of the story for kid? "If you ask for candy and Dad says no, just pitch a fit and you'll even-tually get what you want."

Fib a Little

Hey, what's one more fairy tale to a kid who thinks Hansel and Gretel live around the corner? "I'm sorry, sweetie, but that purple cereal is bad for little bears. Teddy will be mad if you bring it home."

School-Agers (Ages 5 to 8)

By the time they hit school, kids can spot the black-haired babe or heavy-breathing metal face on a cereal box 500 yards away. Worse, they can read: "Look, Mom! If we buy the Swamp Green Crunchy Roasted Sugar Morsels, I can get a genuine ancient Chinese sword for only $14.99!"

That means your survival strategies have to get a little more sophisticated:

Involve Them

You still don't want to open the field up to "anything goes," but there's no reason an 8-year-old can't choose the kind of apple or soup she likes best. Kids this age want to be involved in the process, and it's a good learning experience to explain to them how you choose one product over another, or how advertising is targeted to at kids.

Negotiate

I once sat on a union negotiating team. We were all rank amateurs compared with my 7-year-old daughter.

Kids this age rely on the cruelest negotiating tactics of all: Confuse the competition, and wear them down. Knowing full well that your brain cells are shriveling at an alarming rate, your son will indignantly insist, "But Mom, remember last Tuesday, just before I got into the

QUICK ⬛ *PAINLESS*

Sort the groceries as you buy them: cans in one corner of the cart, frozen foods in another, the produce all in one place. This makes it easier on the checker and the bagger, and can save you a minute or two in the checkout lane.

Want to know in a flash how much sugar a food really has? Just remember this: 4 grams of sugar equals a teaspoon. So a cereal with 16 grams of sugar has 4 teaspoons of the stuff in one serving. No wonder your kid likes it!

bath and when you and Daddy were fighting about the phone bill? I asked if we could buy chocolate cookies next week and you said we could. You promised! Please! Pretty please?"

Fortunately, most kids this age also understand that negotiation is a two-way street. Your best strategy is that of any good negotiator: Know your bottom line, and stick to it.

My kids start out begging for something that has 14 pounds of various food dyes and a million grams of sugar. I counter with shredded wheat. They counteroffer with something that's pastel and has a thousand grams of sugar. I respond with toasted oats. Finally, I "reluctantly" agree to something that's lightly sweetened and whole grain.

Older School-Agers (Ages 9 to 12)

Finally. They're old enough not only to quit pleading and whining (at least most of the time), but also to actually help you shop. Your best strategies:

Divide and Conquer

A friend of ours assigns each of her 11-year-old children a section of the store. "It only works, though, if the kids are familiar enough with what you buy usually—otherwise they don't have a clue what they are looking for," she says. "I usually do the produce and meat aisles, which are more dependent on getting the right quantity and comparing prices. I send the kids to do the other, generally split up by dry goods and dairy/frozen.

"When we are planning for a hectic week, I make three shopping lists. Otherwise, I just tell them a few things and send them off and then send them back again—they love the race idea." She admits she's even given checkout aisle treats to the kid who comes back with the right things in the shortest amount of time, a tactic she describes as "tacky" but effective.

Of course, this strategy should be used only with children who are old enough and responsible enough to thoroughly understand safety. You don't want to send a 5-year-old off into the dairy section, only to have him walk out the door with some overly friendly stranger. Our friend also doesn't send her kids off in large department stores or warehouse stores, where it's easy for even older children to get lost.

Let Your Kids Do the Walking

If you have a store within easy walking or biking distance, you can send your kids out to pick up a loaf of bread, a quart of milk, or the Sunday paper. A 10-year-old can go with a sibling or friend; a child older than 11 can go by herself.

Do be aware, says another friend of ours, that your child may spend the change on candy—a trade-off most parents can probably live with.

Needless to say, this approach also applies only to children who are old and responsible enough to heed safety rules.

IF YOU'RE SO INCLINED

One way to get your kid more interested in shopping is to help him plan a dinner menu with some of his favorite healthful foods. Then he can help you shop for the ingredients, and, finally, help prepare and cook them.

Congratulations! You and your kids survived the supermarket shopping trip in one piece. Make a date to do something just plain fun together: chase grasshoppers, make snow angels, play a game of hopscotch or basketball.

Teens (Ages 13 to 18)

The great thing is that you don't have to take them shopping with you anymore; they're old enough to stay home. Even better, if you play your cards right, you can stay home.

Whatever terror parents feel when their children first get behind the wheel has to be at least partly alleviated by the negotiating room: "Sure, you can have the car all day tomorrow. But only if you pick up a couple of things on your way home from school. Let's see, where did I put that list…"

If you do expect your teenager to shop, keep your list short and very specific. The fact that there is more than one brand or size of chicken broth just isn't very high on the list of things a 15-year-old girl thinks about.

Getting Time on Your Side

	The Old Way	The Lazy Way
Making a list	15 minutes	10 minutes
Reading a food label	1 minute	15 seconds
Buying staples	15 minutes	Already did it
Shopping	45 minutes	20 minutes, when kids help
Going through checkout	5 minutes	3 to 4 minutes
Figuring out how much sugar's in Toasted Crunchies	1 minute	10 seconds

Plan Now, Save Later

Building a healthy diet for your family is a lot easier when you work from a blueprint.

The time to decide what you're all having for dinner is not when you walk in the door after work, tired and in a bad mood because Junior just spilled raspberry juice on your newly cleaned shirt. At the very least, decide the night before what the kids will take in their lunches, and in the morning what you plan to fix for dinner tonight.

Even better, draw up a week's worth of menus before you grocery shop. Don't get overly rigid about it—you don't want to commit to broccoli on Wednesday if the store has a killer sale on asparagus—but do scribble a rough outline: Monday, meat; Tuesday, soup; Wednesday, go out to eat; Thursday, pasta and vegetables; and so on.

MEAL PLANNING, 1-2-3

Here's a trio of strategies that can make menu planning easier.

1. Create "standing" menus or family traditions: Tuesday and Thursday are always vegetarian nights, you always go

IF YOU'RE SO

INCLINED

For fun, scribble the daily or weekly menu, restaurant style, on a board with erasable marker. It'll serve as a quick reminder of what you need to pull out of the freezer, and will stop those "what's for dinner?" questions.

out to eat on Wednesday, your son makes his famous spaghetti on Fridays.

2. Figure out who's going to be home. You should try to eat together as a family whenever possible, but that's not always practical. Plan on light, quick, adjustable meals (sandwiches, popcorn, cheese and crackers and fruit, or whatever) on the days when one of you works late or the kids have evening activities.

3. Enlist your kids' help. If they're young, they can at least choose whether they want chicken or pasta tomorrow night. If they're older, consider assigning each of them one night a week when they get to plan the meal (after you explain why jelly beans are not an acceptable dinner). Once they're about 10, they can not only plan dinner, but also cook it (with supervision, of course).

Now that you've got the foundation in place, here are some ideas to get you started in building healthy meals and snacks.

BREAKFAST, PURE AND SIMPLE

The nutrition experts' recipe for breakfast includes some complex carbohydrates (such as bread, cereal, or fruit), some protein (milk, egg, the chicken left over from last night's dinner), and a little fat (some cream cheese on that bagel). The carbs give your kids a boost of energy, while the protein and fat keep the food in their tummies longer, helping them avoid the late-morning "blahs."

See Chapter 3, "A Chop in Time Saves Nine," for ideas on how to make breakfast easier by having everything prepared the night before. As for what to serve, here are some ideas:

- Bread or bagels with peanut butter or cream cheese, and cantaloupe or peaches.

- Rice cakes and yogurt.

- Last night's leftover pizza or roasted chicken, with fruit.

- Leftover soup, and toast.

- Leftover noodles, reheated in the microwave and tossed with a little cottage cheese and some fresh or canned pineapple chunks.

- Leftover rice, reheated in a bit of milk, with a dash of cinnamon and a handful of raisins.

- A bowl of oatmeal or another whole-grain hot cereal, with milk and a little maple syrup, honey, or brown sugar.

- Frozen whole-grain waffle, with fruit and a small slice of cheese.

- Scrambled eggs or an omelet (see recipes in chapters 11 and 12), with cut-up fruit.

- A tortilla (preferably whole wheat), warmed and wrapped around scrambled eggs and a chopped tomato.

- Blueberry muffins (recipe on page 176), with a little sliced turkey breast or a slice of cheese.

A COMPLETE WASTE OF TIME

The 3 Worst Things to Do with Breakfast:

1. Skip it. Your kids will be hungry and distracted by mid-morning.

2. Define it as a doughnut and soft drink. That's sure to induce a mid-morning "crash."

3. Confine it to nothing but eggs, cereal, or toast. C'mon, get creative!

QUICK n▸ PAINLESS

A frozen juice box makes an ideal ice pack for your kid's lunch. Place it under or over any foods that need to be kept cold. By lunchtime, it will be thawed but still chilly.

LOW-EFFORT LUNCHES

If your kid is in preschool day care, lunch is taken care of. If your children are in school, you can always give them money to buy lunch. But, while hot school lunches are nutritious enough, a lot of kids don't like them, or at least don't like what's being served on a given day.

If you pack their lunches or they pack their own, the biggest problem is boredom. Peanut butter and jelly day after day just doesn't cut it after a while.

So mix it up a bit. Try to pack something besides sandwiches.

Here are some lunch ideas. Those marked with an asterisk must be kept hot or cold. Use an insulated jar for hot foods or cold liquids (follow the manufacturer's warnings and directions). For cold foods, an insulated lunch bag, plus an ice pack, should suffice.

Monday
- Vanilla yogurt*
- Fruit (whole strawberries are yummy)
- Handful of sunflower seeds
- Juice*

Tuesday
- Breadsticks or crackers
- Apple
- Two chunks of cheese (Cheddar or Swiss)*
- Carrot or celery sticks*
- Juice*

Wednesday

- Small bag of cereal-based snack mix, or leftover popcorn
- Hard-cooked egg*
- Fruit
- Milk (buy at school)

Thursday

- Peanut butter and jelly sandwich
- Cut-up raw vegetables (red peppers, broccoli, carrots)*
- Milk (buy at school)

Friday

- Low-fat corn chips
- Small can of bean dip
- Fruit salad*
- Milk (buy at school)

STREAMLINED SNACKS

The easiest way to deal with snacks is to set the rules beforehand. For a start, that means setting snack times, and deciding which snacks are OK to eat in unlimited amounts (generally those that are very low in calories), and which ones are portion-controlled. See Chapter 10, "Smooth Sailing—No More Mealtime Mutiny," for more on this.

YOU'LL THANK YOURSELF LATER

Plan ahead for that harried day when your kid forgets his lunch (or lunch money). Have him keep "emergency" lunch supplies in his locker: cereal and rice milk (don't forget the spoon), canned tuna salad and crackers, or other staples.

QUICK n' PAINLESS

Even the little ones can serve themselves snacks. Put a cracker box in a drawer or cupboard your toddler can reach. She'll have fun opening the box and finding the snack.

Portion-Controlled Snacks

- Seasoned croutons
- Breadsticks
- Crackers
- Graham crackers
- Fig bars
- Dried fruit
- Fruit juice
- Pretzels
- Breakfast cereal, or a cereal snack mix
- Sweet or savory rice cakes
- Breakfast cereal
- Fresh fruit

Eat-All-You-Want Snacks

- Carrot sticks
- Celery sticks
- Vegetable juice
- Cherry tomatoes
- Cucumber slices

DINNER IN MINUTES

Getting the evening meal together can be a hassle, but not if you draw inspiration from the recipes in this book, or from Chapter 4, "Assembly Only Required." Here are even more ideas to get you started.

- Spaghetti tossed with bottled pasta sauce and chopped canned clams. Serve with a salad or green vegetable.

- Baked potatoes topped with leftover spaghetti sauce (page 168), Four-Bean Chili (page 172), or mild salsa and a dab of sour cream.

- Pancakes. They're not just for breakfast. Make them thinner than usual, and top them with a ladleful of stew.

- Deli or carryout roast chicken, accompanied by mashed potatoes (you can use the frozen ones) and a green vegetable or salad.

- "Glop." This is a favorite at my house: a mixture of extra-lean ground beef or ground turkey, diced baking potatoes (or frozen hash browns or leftover french fries), chopped onion, canned or frozen corn, and whatever seasonings I feel like adding. Brown the meat, then cook everything together in a big skillet.

FARMERS MARKET FAVORITES

In the summer, the kids and I go to the Saturday farmers market. I've appointed them the "tasters"; they can tell me if the green beans, or peaches, or apples, are worth buying. They haven't steered me wrong yet.

When the weather's hot and the mood languid, basing a meal on produce from the farmers market really hits the spot.

IF YOU'RE SO INCLINED

How do you make sure your 17-year-old son doesn't demolish that pizza you're saving for tomorrow night? Label it. Make up a bunch of "Hands Off" labels, and stick them on foods that are off limits.

The Lazy Way

Dinner's over and the dishes are cleared. Now, how about an old-fashioned family evening? Play a game of checkers, chess, Scrabble, or cards.

Here are some of our favorite fast, easy summer meals. All are vegetarian, but if you want to add some meat, feel free.

- Corn on the cob, sliced tomatoes, and bread
- Asparagus, bread, cheese, and strawberries for dessert
- Hash browns, green beans, and apricots for dessert
- Steamed snow peas and an omelet
- Falafel in pita pockets, accompanied by plenty of raw veggies—carrots, zucchini, whatever's in season (Note: Instant mixes for the chick-pea croquettes called falafel, or falafil, are available in natural-food stores and many supermarkets. Just add water and fry.)
- A giant salad of lettuce, tomatoes, cucumbers, radishes, and sunflower seeds, with some biscuits or cornbread on the side
- A pizza made with store-bought crust topped with fresh basil, thinly sliced, seeded tomatoes, and a sprinkling of mozzarella

Getting Time on Your Side

	The Old Way	The Lazy Way
Planning menus	10 minutes daily	30 minutes weekly
Serving toddlers snacks	5 minutes	Let them do it
Cooking meat for dinner	15 minutes	Skip it
Making spaghetti sauce	30 minutes	Open the jar
Making falafel	30 minutes	10 minutes
Running your kid's lunch to school when he forgets	30 minutes	No need

Chapter ten

Smooth Sailing—No More Mealtime Mutiny

I once watched a red-faced mom try to hurriedly leave a toy store with her toddler, who was in the throes of a tantrum. The young, obviously childless cashier rolled her eyes. "No child of mine," she pontificated. I quietly snickered and thought, "Oh, just wait." And then realized I sounded like my mom.

Non-parents know exactly how parents should "control" their kids. Those of us who are parents, on the other hand, often find ourselves groping our way through a fog. We nudge, praise, nag, and discipline—and pray our kids catch on before they're 35 and have kids of their own.

Then we promptly declare a dictatorship as soon as we sit down at the dinner table. Next to potty training, getting kids to eat "right"—or at all—ranks near the top of the list of things we parents think we can and should control—and, of course, cannot.

The good news, say most pediatricians and nutrition experts, is that we can relax. Kids have an "off and on" eating style that drives adults buggy, but most manage to get the nutrition they need despite our best efforts to cram food down their throats.

On the other hand, you do have to set and enforce some food and mealtime rules. Otherwise, you'll quickly feel like an unpaid short-order cook.

THE NO. 1 RULE TO REMEMBER

Ellyn Satter, a dietitian who wrote a couple of classic books on feeding children (see Appendix B, "If You Really Want More, Read These"), summed up the golden rule of feeding, which has been widely repeated by childhood nutrition experts:

> Parents are responsible for which food is offered and how it's offered. Children are responsible for how much and even whether they eat.

Adopt this "rule" in your household, and mealtimes will suddenly go a lot smoother. If your daughter chooses to have four helpings of mashed potatoes and your son won't eat his beans...it's their choice. On the other hand, if your son wants to snack morning, noon, and night...you don't have to let him do it.

HOW TO HANDLE...

Picky Eaters

Kids are creatures of habit (aren't we all?). They balk at unknown things, including that nutritious vegetable you know as spinach but they suspect is pond scum. Here are some ways to help counteract this:

IF YOU'RE SO INCLINED

For young kids, make a game of trying different foods. When they taste something new, ask them to draw a face describing how they feel about it. (Really young kids can pick from smiley or frowney faces you draw; older kids can write down words.)

- The "green eggs" rule (with credit—or is it apologies?—to the late, great Dr. Seuss). Whenever we serve a new food, we ask the kids to take a bite. If they don't like it, fine; if they do, great. If it's a food we're 99 percent sure they're going to hate, we don't force the issue.

- The one-yucky-thing rule. A friend of ours who raised three kids said her dinnertime rule was that you were allowed to turn down one food at the table. This inspired the kids to reflect on their food choices: "Hmm, let's see, broccoli's OK sometimes, but peas are truly disgusting. So I'll try a little broccoli."

- The one-yummy-thing rule. This is a rule for parents. At every meal, you should serve at least one food you know your kid will eat, even if it's just bread or rice. That's only fair. This does not mean you cook a second meal for your kids. If you do that, how will they ever have an incentive to try new foods?

- The try-try-again rule. Nutrition experts say kids often have to be introduced to a new food 5 or 10 different times before they'll eat it. (P.S. Offering it to them 10 times during the same meal does not count.)

The Kid Who Wants to Eat All the Time

First off, you probably need to get a handle on why she's eating all the time. Is she eating out of boredom? Find something else for her to do.

QUICK ⬛ PAINLESS

Some dietitian/moms I've talked to suggest serving dessert right along with the meal, rather than after, so it loses its special importance. I've never had the nerve to try this, but moms who've done it claim their kids eat the dessert and their other food.

YOU'LL THANK YOURSELF LATER

If your child seems to have a truly serious problem with food— vomiting, constant diarrhea, an obsession with calories or body image, or constant bingeing— call your pediatrician. There may be an underlying emotional or physical problem you need to address.

Is he eating because he's about ready to go through another growth spurt? You can bet this is the case if you've just spent a fortune on his new school clothes.

Or are your kids eating what looks like too often to you but is actually normal? The average 7- to 10-year-old needs about the same number of calories (2,200 a day) as the average active woman, but has a much smaller stomach. Obviously, this means the child needs to eat more often. Generally, three meals a day plus a couple of snack times is about right.

Teenage boys are especially notorious for sending grocery bills skyrocketing. This isn't surprising, since the average boy age 11 to 18 needs anywhere from 2,500 to 2,800 calories a day. A couple of carrot sticks just isn't going to cut it as a snack. (Girls have steadier calorie needs, about 2,200 from late childhood through adolescence.)

The "I'm Not Hungry" Kid

Why hammer away at your kid if he really isn't hungry? He may just eat twice as much at the next meal. On the other hand, if he's distracted and would rather play than eat, that's his problem, too. If he comes up to you a half hour later and complains that he's hungry, tell him no food until snack time or the next meal. He'll be mad, but he's not going to starve before 7 a.m. tomorrow, and he'll quickly get the point that Mommy and Daddy's drive-through window is closed for the day.

- Watch what she's drinking. If she drinks tons of milk and/or juice, she may be filling up between meals. Sometimes, water is the perfect beverage.

- Watch the snack times. Obviously, if your son eats a huge snack at 4:30 p.m., he's pretty unlikely to want to eat much dinner at 5:30.

Kids Who Want You to Follow Their Schedule

Your daughter says she's not hungry at dinner, toys with her food, and leaves most of it on the plate. An hour later, she's begging for a sandwich. Or she trades away most of her lunch at school, eats a cracker when she gets home, and then wants a huge snack 20 minutes before dinner.

It's true that eating three meals a day is a cultural thing. No reason we shouldn't eat two meals a day, or six. However, you have to bring some order to mealtimes, unless you want to open a short-order restaurant and feed your kids on demand. (If you do own a restaurant, you don't have to read this part.) Our solution is to allow the kids to snack at certain times of the day. We have a no-snacks-after-4-p.m. rule. You'll need to adjust your rules according to your family's circumstances. For example, if your children are in day care and you don't pick them up until 6 p.m., it makes sense to give them a snack when they get home, and consider it part of their dinner.

Whatever rules you set, enforce them. Most experts agree: Whether or not your child eats at a given meal or snack time is up to her, but setting mealtimes is your job.

Reassure your daughter that when she grows up and gets her own apartment, she can eat hot dogs at midnight and breakfast at noon whenever she wants. At least until she has kids of her own…

QUICK **n** *PAINLESS*

Here's how to quickly reckon serving sizes for young kids:

- For ages 3 and under, 1 tablespoon of food per year of age.

- For ages 4 to 5, about two-thirds of recommended Food Guide Pyramid serving sizes (see Chapter 7, " Right Bites: Foods that Make the Grade").

- For ages 5 and up, Food Pyramid serving sizes.

Note that these are only guidelines, and as this book was being written, the government was setting standard serving sizes for children.

The Kid Who Shuns Breakfast

Not all kids like the idea of breakfast in the morning. Unfortunately, skipping breakfast will make it much harder for your child to concentrate in his morning classes. If your kid's one of those slow-starters in the morning, keep breakfast very simple: a bowl of cereal, a container of yogurt. Or, if your school serves breakfast, just let him wait and buy it there.

If he's the type who's up and whistling at dawn (egad), he may want breakfast before your eyes are fully open. If he's old enough, let him help himself to fruit, yogurt, or cereal.

The Kid Who Wants to Eat Only "Junk"

Again, this could be a family problem. If you live on fast food carryout, why should your kid be any different? Make high-calorie, sugar- or fat-laden foods a rarity, rather than the routine, in your household.

- Forget health—play up vanity. Tell young kids broccoli and skim milk will help make them stronger or make their hair shinier. For teens, do a little research to dig up articles on how their favorite movie star, musician or athlete eats (and make sure the object of adoration does, indeed, eat healthfully).

- On the other hand, because kids, especially teenage boys, do require so many calories, they can "afford" more empty calories than their aging parents can. If your kid is basically eating right and is active, why yell over a few french fries and a milk shake?

YOU'LL THANK YOURSELF LATER

Sometimes kids may not eat much because the portions look overwhelming to them. Remember to keep things on a kid-size scale. Cut a sandwich in four triangles, cut meats and vegetables into small pieces, and serve things on small plates.

Kids Who Try "Fad" Diets

Teenagers experiment with their clothes and hair, and engage in piercing rituals that make adults shudder. So, why wouldn't they experiment with food?

Vegetarianism

Actually, this is not a "fad" diet, but an age-old eating style that a fair number of teenagers embrace, often for ethical reasons. As a group, vegetarians tend to stay healthier and live longer than those of us who eat meat. (Researchers aren't sure if it's diet alone that makes the difference, or whether vegetarians lean toward healthier lifestyles in general.)

So, if you're a meat eater, don't go ballistic when your teen suddenly announces he won't eat anything with a "face." You may already be eating meatless meals a couple of times a week anyway. The rest of the time, your teen can either make his own meal, or just eat everything except the meat.

It is important, however, that a vegetarian diet (like any diet) be well balanced among the various food groups. If your teen is a vegan (doesn't eat any animal products, including dairy or egg), it's not a bad idea for her to take a calcium supplement, and maybe a multivitamin. If she drinks rice or soy-based beverages instead of milk, she should choose those fortified with calcium and vitamin D.

Athletic or Weight-Loss Miracle Diets

Boy, if I had a dollar for every diet that's come and gone...The good news here is that many of these diets

A COMPLETE WASTE OF TIME

The 3 Worst Vegetarian Diets:

1. Nothing but salads.

2. The french fry–macaroni and cheese regimen.

3. The chocolate chip cookie diet.

and supplements are more silly than dangerous, and most kids (and adults) quickly grow bored with them. The bad news is that an ultra-restrictive diet, an unproven supplement, or a full-blown obsession with calories or weight can indeed be harmful.

Again, there's not much you can do to control what goes in your kid's stomach, especially if she's a teenager. You can do your best to educate her about proper food choices (for example, why skim milk is a much better bet than diet soda), and to set a good example. If you feel a teacher or coach is encouraging bad eating habits, have a talk with the adult.

Once again: If your child of any age seems to have an abnormal fixation with food—whether it's eating way too little or way too much—call the pediatrician.

Preaching

Dinnertime should not be a time to argue. In other words, whichever member of the family has chosen to shun meat (or eat it) or has decided desserts are a mortal sin should not preach to the rest of the family. At least not at the table.

Mind Your Peas and Q's

As a parent, you're in charge of table manners. If you aren't, mealtimes can turn into fiascoes. Here are some rules we follow in our household.

- Eat now, play later. We insist that when the kids are at the table, they eat, rather than play, pet the cats, or have spitting fights with their juice.

YOU'LL THANK YOURSELF LATER

From the time they're little, explain the role of advertising to your kids and, as much as possible, limit their exposure to TV ads. Let's face it, nobody will ever spend as much money promoting bananas and lettuce as they do giant cheeseburgers and candy bars.

- Eat at the table. This not only keeps the house tidier, but also discourages kids from running around with food in their mouth—a practice that can be harmful, especially with foods on sticks, such as frozen pops. It also discourages "mindless" eating; that is, eating a bag of chips while you watch TV. (One exception: As a treat, we do occasionally let the kids have popcorn and a movie in the family room.)

- The veggie libel law. Our kids do not have to eat any food they don't like, but they also are not allowed to loudly pronounce the food "gross," make rude noises, or question the mental capabilities of anyone who chooses to eat it. This rule also extends to my husband's pronouncements on tofu.

- And where would we be without that golden oldie: Don't talk with your mouth full! Which leads us to…

SAFETY SENSE

Choking on food isn't just something parents nag about. It has happened, with tragic results. (We once lost a darling neighbor boy when a piece of hot dog lodged in his throat.) For a start, parents and caregivers should know the Heimlich maneuver and child CPR. That aside, the most basic safety rule is to feed kids age-appropriate foods. Young children often can't, or don't, chew foods the way they should, and can easily choke on hard foods that are the right size to lodge in their windpipes.

QUICK ⬛ PAINLESS

If your toddler or preschooler is more interested in playing than eating, remove her from the table and put her on the floor to play. This reinforces the idea that playing and eating are separate activities.

Don't Feed Babies:

- Honey. Their stomachs cannot neutralize any botulism spores present. Honey is safe for toddlers and older kids.

- Mint or mint candy. Its strong flavor may make a baby feel like he's choking.

Don't Feed Babies or Toddlers:

- Chunky peanut butter (and feed smooth peanut butter only in small amounts and with supervision)

- Fruits with large seeds, pits, or thick skins (peel and pit them first)

Don't Feed Babies, Toddlers, or Young Preschoolers (Under the Age of 4):

- Any hard, rounded foods that could lodge in their throat: hot dogs, carrot sticks, celery sticks, grapes, hard candies, broccoli florets, popcorn, etc.

- Hard, smooth foods that must be chewed with a grinding motion (for example, nuts and peanuts). In fact, the American Academy of Pediatricians recommends not serving whole peanuts to children under the age of 7.

- Chewing gum. The child should be old enough (usually age 4 or 5) to truly understand she should not swallow it. If kids swallow too much gum, it can literally gum up their intestines.

YOU'LL THANK YOURSELF LATER

Peanut allergies are on the rise, and some allergists theorize that babies' earlier exposure to the sticky stuff may be a contributing factor. Don't be in a hurry to introduce babies or young toddlers to peanut butter.

Don't Feed to a Kid of Any Age:

- Any food that makes the child wheeze, break out in a rash, vomit, or that seems to constipate him or give him diarrhea. He may have an allergy or intolerance to it. Stop feeding it to him and consult your pediatrician.

QUICK  PAINLESS

The good side to gum is that it's a quick way for kids to "brush." Dentists say chewing sugarless gum after meals can help keep plaque from forming.

Getting Time on Your Side

	The Old Way	The Lazy Way
Getting through dinner	1 hour	30 minutes
Getting your son to eat green beans	Good luck	Why should he?
Making snacks	3 hours a day	15 minutes
Pleading with your 3-year-old to quit playing and eat	10 minutes	0 minutes
Getting your vegetarian daughter to eat meat	Years, if ever	It's her choice
Breakfast	15 minutes	5 minutes

Part 4

No-Sweat Healthy Eating

Are You Too Lazy to Read No-Sweat Healthy Eating?

1 You swear the last time you made a stir-fry, it took three years to cut up all the vegetables. ☐ yes ☐ no

2 You overheard your daughter telling her Barbie she'd better eat her carrots or the vegetable monster is going to eat her. ☐ yes ☐ no

3 Your skillet has cobwebs hanging from the handle. ☐ yes ☐ no

Mix and Match in Minutes

The preparation times given for the recipes in chapters 11 through 17 are based on the assumption that most of the ingredients have already been prepared. Who wants to chop up tons of vegetables on a busy weeknight? Instead, take advantage of the vast assortment of ready-prepared ingredients from the produce department, salad bar, and aisles of the supermarket.

Chopped onions? Buy them frozen. Minced garlic and ginger? They come in jars. Pesto? You'll find it in the refrigerator section. Broccoli florets, carrot sticks, and sliced pineapple? They're in the produce department or on the salad bar. And so on.

Of course, you do pay more for such convenience. You can save money—and in at least some cases, get better flavor—by chopping up fruits and vegetables yourself. But do it all at once, right after you've brought them home, or when you have a few spare minutes over the weekend. Store them in resealable plastic bags in the crisper drawer.

You've made it through dinner, and everyone's happy. How about a round of funny food rhymes? See how many words the kids can think up that rhyme with carrot. Or beet. Bet you can't think of a rhyme with broccoli...

The Lazy Way

With all the ingredients already chopped up, a stir-fry is just minutes away.

One of you loves eggplant; everyone else loathes it. One of you eats chile peppers by the handful; the other cringes if there's a jalapeno within 40 feet. One kid devours anything that doesn't eat him first; the other kid dissects every dish with surgical precision, looking for a microscopic bit of garlic that might have escaped his scrutiny.

It's inevitable, of course. Anytime you get a bunch of different personalities together, family or not, they're never going to agree on everything. But differing tastes can make cooking a real pain in the posterior.

When it was just my husband and me, cooking was fairly fun. While we have different tastes, we had a lot of common ground as well (we both adore spicy Asian food, for starters). Once we tossed two more opinions into the stew, macaroni and cheese suddenly took on more appeal.

That's why it pays to develop a repertoire of "mix and match" dishes, simple recipes that easily adjust to varying tastes. This way, you can pretend you're preparing two or even three "different" meals, while cooking only one.

THE RECIPES

What makes these recipes mix and match is that they start with very basic ingredients—egg, rice, bread, meat, and potatoes—that nearly everyone likes. It's the extras that "customize" them.

Asian Scramble

This egg dish is good with sliced raw tomatoes, a tossed green salad, oven-fried potatoes, and/or fruit.

▓ **Preparation Time:** About 5 minutes

▓ **Cooking Time:** About 5 to 6 minutes

▓ **Servings:** 4

8 eggs (or 4 eggs and 1 cup egg substitute)

$^1/_2$ pound cooked, shelled medium shrimp

1 cup frozen peas, defrosted (or 1 cup chopped fresh tomato)

$^1/_2$ cup fresh bean sprouts (or substitute canned, drained chopped water chestnuts or bamboo shoots)

2 tablespoons canola or vegetable oil

$^1/_4$ cup chopped regular or green onions

1 teaspoon soy sauce (optional)

Salt and pepper to taste

1 Put the eggs in a bowl and whisk lightly.

2 Rinse the bean sprouts under hot water. Then stir the shrimp, peas, and bean sprouts into the eggs.

3 Heat the oil in a nonstick frying pan. Add the onions and cook for a few minutes over medium heat, stirring occasionally, until they soften.

4 Add the egg mixture. Cook the eggs, moving the eggs around with a spatula or wooden spoon, and folding and lifting them as they set.

5 Season the eggs with soy sauce, salt, and pepper. Spoon onto individual plates and serve hot.

QUICK ⬤ PAINLESS

Looking for a super-quick alternative to pasta or rice? Try polenta. This boiled cornmeal is sold as fat "sausages" in the produce department and on the shelves. Just cut off slices, heat them in a skillet or the microwave, and top with anything you like, from maple syrup to bottled spaghetti sauce.

Southwest Scramble

You can make this dish fairly bland for the children, and much spicier for the adults. For example, add chopped garlic and chopped green chile peppers (fresh or canned) to the adult portion.

This dish is good with a tossed salad, fruit (especially mangos or melon), and/or sliced raw tomatoes. You also can stuff the eggs into flour tortillas for a quick breakfast, lunch, or dinner burrito.

Preparation Time: 5 minutes

Cooking Time: 5 to 6 minutes

Servings: 4

8 eggs (or 4 eggs and 1 cup egg substitute)

$1/4$ cup nonfat or low-fat milk

2 teaspoons chili powder

2 tablespoons canola or olive oil

$1/2$ cup Mexican-style low-fat or regular shredded or crumbled cheese

$3/4$ cup mild bottled or fresh salsa

One 16-ounce can refried beans, heated

Flour or corn tortillas, warmed

1 Put the eggs, milk, and chili powder in a bowl and whisk lightly.

2 Heat the oil in a nonstick frying pan. Add the egg mixture. Cook the eggs, moving them around with a spatula or wooden spoon, and folding and lifting them as they set.

IF YOU'RE SO INCLINED

Fresh salsa beats the heck out of bottled salsa for flavor. If your supermarket deli doesn't carry the fresh stuff, you can quickly make your own by chopping onion, tomatoes, cilantro, and maybe a chili pepper, and tossing them together.

3 Stir in the shredded cheese. Continue cooking the eggs until they're set but still moist.

4 Spoon the eggs onto individual plates and top with the salsa.

5 Serve hot, with the refried beans and warm tortillas on the side.

QUICK **n** PAINLESS

Canned refried beans come in assorted flavors and degrees of "fatness" these days. Just spoon them into a bowl and zap them in the microwave to quickly reheat.

Fried Rice

Fried rice does not have to be a side dish. It makes a great main course, accompanied by a salad or fruit.

It's important that the rice be cold; that makes it less likely to stick to the pan.

You can use egg substitute instead of part or all of the whole eggs, or skip the eggs altogether.

Preparation Time: 10 minutes

Cooking Time: 10 minutes

Servings: 10 to 12 as a side dish; 6 as a main course

4 eggs, lightly beaten (optional)

3 tablespoons vegetable oil, divided

1 tablespoon minced garlic

2 teaspoons minced ginger

1 cup chopped onions (regular or green; optional)

6 cups defrosted cooked white rice

One 10-ounce package frozen green peas, or 1 cup chopped red or green peppers

2 cups fresh bean sprouts, rinsed under hot water, or one 6-ounce can sliced water chestnuts, drained

1 cup chopped leftover cooked chicken, pork or beef (optional)

$^1/_4$ cup light teriyaki sauce

Salt and pepper to taste

1 Lightly whisk the eggs.

2 Heat $1^1/_2$ tablespoons of the oil in a wok or a deep, non-stick frying pan over medium heat. Add the eggs and cook, stirring, until set. Remove to a paper plate.

IF YOU'RE SO INCLINED

You can make a big batch of the fried rice base (the rice, onion, and egg), then divide it into resealable freezer bags, and freeze it for another day. Just toss it into the skillet or wok and add whatever vegetables and meats you have handy.

3 Reheat the wok (if necessary, wipe it out first) and heat $1^1/_2$ tablespoons oil. Add the garlic and onion and cook a few minutes until softened.

4 Add the rice. Stir-fry over medium-high heat, moving the rice quickly with a wooden spoon.

5 Add the vegetables and the chicken or meat. Stir-fry a few minutes until heated through.

6 Stir in the sauce, and season the rice with salt and pepper. Serve hot.

QUICK n' PAINLESS

The "large piece" trick: My son hates biting into garlic. The rest of us love the stuff. Instead of mincing the garlic, I slice it. We get the garlic flavor and he can easily pick the pieces out of his food.

Stir-Fried Chicken with Vegetables

To "stir-fry" means to move small pieces of uncooked food quickly over a high heat. Although this kind of cooking is easiest in a wok, any well-seasoned or nonstick frying pan with deep sides will do. If your family is watching your fat intake, substitute chicken broth for the oil or use nonstick cooking spray and a nonstick frying pan.

- **Preparation Time:** 5 to 10 minutes
- **Cooking Time:** 5 to 8 minutes
- **Servings:** 4 to 6

2 tablespoons canola or vegetable oil

1 teaspoon minced ginger

$1^1/_2$ pounds skinless chicken breast tenders or stir-fry strips

Two 8-ounce packages washed and trimmed snap peas, or 5 cups of another vegetable of your choice (such as asparagus, cauliflower or broccoli florets, thin carrot sticks, or mixed vegetables)

One 6-ounce can sliced water chestnuts, drained

1 cup sliced fresh mushrooms (optional)

$^1/_3$ cup bottled light (reduced-sodium) stir-fry sauce

1 cup sliced almonds (optional)

1 Heat the oil in a wok or nonstick frying pan. Add the ginger and cook for just a few seconds.

2 Add the chicken and stir-fry for about 2 minutes.

IF YOU'RE SO INCLINED

To bring out their flavor, toast the almonds before you start stir-frying. Toast them in the dry wok or skillet over medium heat, shaking the pan. Watch them carefully; they burn fast. As soon as they're lightly browned, pour them onto a napkin or plate.

3 Add the pea pods (or other vegetables), the water chestnuts, and the mushrooms. Continue cooking, moving the food around in the pan, until the chicken is cooked through.

4 Add the sauce and cook until it's heated through. Stir in the almonds.

5 Serve hot over cooked white rice.

YOU'LL THANK YOURSELF LATER

If your older kid has a favorite food that the rest of you don't necessarily eat, make it her responsibility to keep track of when it's time to buy more and jot it down on the shopping list.

Orange and White Potato Wedges

Sweet potatoes are very nutritious, but not all kids like them. This recipe calls for a "mix-and-match" combo of sweet and white potatoes, but can be made with all sweet potatoes, or all white potatoes.

- **Preparation Time:** 10 minutes
- **Baking Time:** 1 hour
- **Servings:** 6

   Olive oil–flavored nonstick cooking spray

   3 medium sweet potatoes

   3 medium baking potatoes

   1 tablespoon cumin seeds (optional)

   Chili powder to taste (or, substitute seasoned salt, onion powder, curry powder, or whatever your family likes)

   Salt and pepper to taste

   Salsa, ketchup, and/or soy sauce for dipping

1 Preheat the oven to 425°F. Spray a cookie sheet (preferably nonstick) with the cooking spray.

2 Wash the potatoes. Using a small sharp knife, cut the potatoes in half lengthwise. Then set each potato cut side down and cut each half again into 2 lengthwise wedges.

3 Arrange the potatoes on the cookie sheet. Spray them generously with cooking spray, and sprinkle with the seasonings.

YOU'LL THANK YOURSELF LATER

When you're choosing sweet potatoes in the market, look for the medium-sized, slender ones, rather than the large ones. They cook faster, and are more tender.

4 Bake the potato wedges in the center of the oven for 1 hour, turning once or twice during the baking time, or until they can be pierced easily with a fork.

5 Serve with salsa, ketchup, or soy sauce.

IF YOU'RE SO
INCLINED

You can serve these potato wedges as a vegetarian main course to three or four, with a salad and fruit. They also are very good as a side dish with turkey.

Getting Time on Your Side

	The Old Way	The Lazy Way
Making three dinners	30 minutes	10 minutes
Slicing beef and vegetables	30 minutes	0 minutes
Chopping garlic and ginger	2 minutes	2 seconds
Picking garlic out of your son's food	3 minutes	1 minute
Getting fried rice (includes time spent driving)	45 minutes	15 minutes
Cooking rice	20 minutes	0 minutes

Meals that Stretch So You Don't Have To

Despite your best efforts, as your kids grow older, it gets increasingly difficult to get everyone to the table at the same time. Suddenly, 5 o'clock rolls around and you realize your daughter's still at soccer practice, your son's saxophone lesson is in an hour, and it's Tuesday, the day your spouse does the accounts and doesn't get home until 8:30.

Everyone's going to want dinner, of course—just not at the same time.

One solution is "accordion meals": Harmonious combinations that stretch to accommodate one person or ten. As long as you have the basic ingredients on hand—eggs, tortillas, pitas, and so on—you can whip up one of something for yourself or 12-somethings for your daughter and her Girl Scout troop. Or better yet, have the ingredients ready so everyone can make their own dinner.

Of course, you can always take the really easy route and just let everyone eat microwave popcorn or a bowl of cereal.

THE RECIPES

All of these meals can be made as individual pieces, so it's easy to serve 1, 6, or 15.

Chicken or Turkey Barbecue Rollups

Wraps are popular with both kids and adults, mainly because they're pretty and a nice change from the usual sandwich. To keep the wraps from falling apart, slice them on the diagonal with a very sharp, non-serrated knife. These are great for box lunches; just be sure to keep them cold.

- **Preparation Time:** 10 minutes
- **Cooking Time:** 0 minutes
- **Servings:** 8

3 tablespoons favorite barbecue sauce

1 cup plain nonfat yogurt or nonfat sour cream

8 regular or whole wheat flour tortillas or wraps (if the wraps are large you might want to cut them in half)

2 cups washed and cut lettuce

1 rotisserie chicken, meat removed and thinly sliced, or $^1/_2$ to $^3/_4$ pound smoked thinly sliced turkey breast

$1^1/_2$ cups sliced red, green, or yellow peppers

$^1/_2$ cup sliced olives or pickles (optional)

1 Combine the barbecue sauce with the yogurt or sour cream; refrigerate.

2 For each wrap, spread about $2^1/_2$ tablespoons of the flavored yogurt over the tortillas. Top with the lettuce.

QUICK **n** PALNLESS

For sandwiches, especially rollups, leaf lettuce is the easiest lettuce to deal with. It's soft and pliable. Romaine is a good second choice, if you remove the center rib.

3 Arrange the chicken or turkey slices evenly over the tortilla in a single layer. Sprinkle with the peppers and olives.

4 Roll up each tortilla tightly and set it, seam side down, on a plate. If you are not serving the rollups immediately, cover them with plastic wrap and refrigerate; they will keep for up to 12 hours.

To make wraps one at a time: Use 1 tortilla, $\frac{1}{4}$ cup lettuce (or 1 large leaf), 2 slices of chicken or turkey, 2 or 3 slices of pepper, and $\frac{1}{4}$ cup sliced olives or pickles

For some fun, let the kids choose what to stuff into wraps. They may come up with some wild combinations, but hey, cooking is supposed to be creative.

The Lazy Way

A COMPLETE WASTE OF TIME

The 3 Worst Things to Do with Eggs:

1. Undercook them. The yolks and whites should be set.

2. Overcook them. They should be moist, not dry.

3. Put whole ones in the microwave: exploding eggs, anyone?

Hearty Two-Cheese Omelet

If you have eggs in the house, you always have dinner close at hand. Serve the omelet with the Orange and White Potato Wedges (page 134), a green salad, or fruit.

This can be made as one large omelet, or as four individual omelets. You can add different fillings, of course, just before folding over the omelet. Try sliced fresh mushrooms, chopped herbs, a little chopped or shredded lean ham, chopped walnuts, or chopped fresh tomato.

Preparation Time: 5 minutes

Cooking Time: 5 to 6 minutes (less for individual omelets)

Servings: 4

8 eggs (or 4 eggs plus 1 cup egg substitute)
3 tablespoons nonfat or low-fat milk
$2^1/_2$ tablespoons olive or canola oil
$^1/_2$ cup chopped onions (optional)
2 tablespoons shredded Cheddar cheese
3 tablespoons creamy, small curd cottage cheese
Salt and pepper to taste

1 Put the eggs and milk in a bowl and whisk lightly.

2 Heat the oil in a nonstick frying pan. Add the onions and cook over medium heat, stirring often, until softened.

3 Add the eggs. As the eggs cook, gently lift the cooked outer edges so that the uncooked eggs flow to the bottom of the pan.

4. When the omelet has begun to set, sprinkle the cheeses in the center, along with any other toppings desired. Sprinkle with salt and pepper.

5. Fold one side of the eggs over to the center, and repeat with the opposite side of the omelet. Slide the omelet onto a plate. Cut it into serving pieces and serve immediately.

To make individual omelets: For each one, use 2 eggs, 1 teaspoon milk, 1 teaspoon oil, 1 tablespoon onion, a very light sprinkling of Cheddar cheese, and a small dab of cottage cheese.

QUICK 🔳 PAINLESS

Not sure which size eggs to buy? Buy large. Cookbook recipes are always designed for large eggs (unless the recipe specifically states otherwise). This means you'll always have the right eggs for both eating and cooking.

Turn these into grilled cheese sandwiches by topping each with a second slice of bread. Coat a nonstick frying pan with butter-flavored cooking spray. Grill the sandwich(es) over medium heat for about 4 minutes, then turn and grill another 4 minutes, or until toasted.

Open-Face Cheese Sandwiches

These are ideal for a quick lunch or for a light dinner, if you add a tossed salad or some fruit.

This is a good recipe for young teenagers to learn to make for themselves, family, and friends. Make sure that you teach them to always use potholders.

Preparation Time: 5 minutes

Cooking Time: 6 minutes

Servings: 6

6 slices whole wheat, raisin, millet, oat, or other bread of your choice

6 slices of Cheddar, American, or Monterey Jack cheese (regular or reduced-fat)

Vegetables (optional): 6 thin red onion slices, 6 thin tomato slices, and/or 6 slices of red or green bell pepper

Alfalfa or radish sprouts (optional)

1 Preheat the oven or toaster oven to 375°F.

2 Arrange the bread slices on a nonstick cookie sheet (or on the toaster oven tray, if you're making 1 or 2 sandwiches). Set the cheese on the bread. Top with the onion, tomato, and/or pepper slices.

3 Bake in the center of the oven for about 6 minutes, or until the cheese melts.

4 Set on individual plates, and sprinkle with the sprouts.

English Muffin Pizzas

These mini-pizzas are ideal for older kids or teenagers to make. If you keep a bunch in the freezer, the kids can heat them up as they need them in the toaster oven or even in the microwave.

- **Preparation time:** 5 minutes
- **Baking Time:** 8 to 10 minutes
- **Servings:** 6

6 English muffins, plain or whole wheat
$^3/_4$ to 1 cup pizza sauce or spaghetti sauce
$1^1/_2$ cups (6 ounces) shredded regular or reduced-fat
    mozzarella
Dried oregano or basil

1 Cut the muffins in half and toast them.

2 Preheat the oven (or toaster oven) to 375°F.

3 Arrange the toasted muffins on a nonstick cookie sheet (or on the toaster oven tray, if you're making just one or two).

4 Spread the muffins with the sauce and top with the cheese. Sprinkle lightly with oregano.

5 Bake the muffin pizzas in the center of the oven for 8 to 10 minutes, or until the cheese has melted and the muffins are hot. Serve immediately.

    To make individual pizzas: Use 1 English muffin, 1 tablespoon sauce, and 1 tablespoon grated cheese for each pizza.

YOU'LL THANK YOURSELF LATER

Always buy mozzarella already shredded. Nearly all the time, you're going to put it in or on something where you want it to melt, so why hassle with shredding it yourself?

Whole Wheat Pita Pizzas

This is basically a variation of the above recipe. Using pita breads, which are larger than English muffins, gives you more flexibility with toppings. Slicing through the pita breads produces two thin rounds, which yields a crisper crust, but that step is optional.

- **Preparation Time:** 5 minutes
- **Baking Time:** 10 minutes
- **Servings:** 6

6 whole wheat or regular pita breads

1 pound shredded part-skim mozzarella cheese

One 14-ounce jar pizza sauce

Dried basil and/or oregano

Toppings: Sliced peppers, sliced fresh mushrooms, sliced lean ham, sliced tomatoes, sliced red onions or chopped green onions, fresh or frozen, thawed spinach, basil leaves

1 Preheat the oven (or toaster oven) to 375°F.

2 Cut through each pita bread to make 2 rounds. Arrange the pita rounds, cut side up, on nonstick cookie sheets (or on a toaster oven tray, if you making just 1 or 2 pizzas).

3 Sprinkle the mozzarella over the pitas. Drizzle with the pizza sauce. (Putting the cheese on the bottom keeps the crust from getting soggy.) Sprinkle with basil and/or oregano.

IF YOU'RE SO INCLINED

Make the pizzas with the toppings you like, then freeze them on a cookie sheet until they're solid. Wrap each in plastic wrap and pop them back into the freezer, ready to be turned into quick lunches or dinner. To heat the pizzas, unwrap them and put them, still frozen, in a toaster oven at 400°F.

4 Arrange toppings of your choice over the cheese and sauce.

5 Bake the pizzas in the center of the oven for 10 minutes or until the cheese has melted.

To make individual pizzas: Top each pita round with about ¼ cup of cheese and 2 tablespoons of pizza sauce.

YOU'LL THANK YOURSELF LATER

Make sure you invest in at least one good-quality nonstick skillet. They're a necessity in the lazy kitchen. They are easy to clean and relatively inexpensive, and allow you to cook with much less fat.

Pita Pockets Stuffed with Beef and Vegetables

Make up a big skillet of the basic beef and veggie mix, then let your kids or spouse reheat the mixture and stuff it into pitas when they're ready to eat.

- **Preparation Time:** 5 minutes
- **Cooking Time:** About 5 minutes
- **Servings:** 6 (12 pita pockets)

1^1/$_2$ pounds boneless beef sirloin, thinly sliced

^{1}/$_4$ cup light (reduced-sodium) teriyaki sauce

Pepper (to taste)

2 tablespoons canola or vegetable oil

3 cups prepared fresh or frozen vegetables of your choice, in small pieces (some suggestions: stir-fry mix, sliced carrots, sliced peppers, fresh washed spinach, fresh tomatoes, sliced or chopped onions)

6 regular or whole wheat pocket pita breads

1. Sprinkle the sliced beef with the teriyaki sauce and the pepper. Set aside.

2. Heat the oil in a wok or in a deep nonstick frying pan. Add the vegetables and cook, stirring, for about 2 minutes. If you're using hard vegetables, such as broccoli or carrots, add a bit of water to the pan to help them "steam."

QUICK ⬭ PAINLESS

To save time, buy the beef already sliced. You should be able to find stir-fry strips—perhaps even already seasoned with teriyaki sauce—in the meat department.

3 Add the beef, and continue to cook, stirring, until the vegetables are cooked through but still crisp, and the beef is no longer pink.

4 Cut the pita breads in half, and lightly warm them in the toaster oven or microwave.

5 Spoon the beef and vegetables into the warm pita halves. Serve hot.

IF YOU'RE SO
INCLINED

You can stuff just about anything into a pita. This is a great way to use up leftovers.

Getting Time on Your Side

	The Old Way	The Lazy Way
Cooking meals at 5, 6, and 8 p.m.	1 hour +	Just cook once
Cooking for busy teenagers	30 minutes	Let them do it
Slicing beef	5 minutes	0 minutes
Shredding mozzarella	5 minutes	0 minutes
Making pizza crusts	$1^1/_2$ hours	2 minutes
Making pizza sauce	20 minutes	0 minutes

Instant Veggie (and Fruit) Stardom

Quick—what foods do adults and kids tussle over the most?

Vegetables!

"My mother had this thing about cooked carrots," says a friend of ours. "She would make them at least once a week, and would force us to eat them. I'd have eaten a hundred of them raw, but she wouldn't serve them that way. To this day, I can't stomach a cooked carrot."

Many of us are veterans of eat-your-veggies battles (my Waterloo was green beans). This may explain why some families seem to go to the other extreme. I've met kids who apparently live on nothing but hot dogs and peanut butter and jelly. I'm curious: Do they somehow absorb vitamin C from the atmosphere?

THE TRUTH ABOUT KIDS AND VEGETABLES

Getting kids to eat veggies actually isn't that hard, but it does require that you keep a few things in mind:

- Children have more sensitive taste buds than adults. Your son doesn't turn up his nose at your stuffed green peppers just to spite you (although that may add to the thrill), but because green peppers taste bitter to him.

- Most kids will eat vegetables, if you give them a chance to. Maybe not a lot of vegetables, and maybe only certain ones. And even kids who don't eat vegetables will usually eat fruit, which is perfectly nutritious.

- Forcing a child to eat vegetables she doesn't like just wastes your time and hers. Now, I hate to sound preachy, but think about this a minute. I hate lima beans. Always have, always will. Never has my husband stood over me and said, "You have to eat your lima beans before you get dessert." Besides the fact that this would endanger his life (nobody stands between me and a brownie), he wouldn't do it because it's silly. What, I'm going to die of malnutrition if I don't eat lima beans? (Of course, there's the fact that he despises lima beans himself, but that's another story.)

So, tell me again: Why does your son have to eat his peas?

IF YOU'RE SO
INCLINED

Even if you have only a small balcony, you can easily grow cherry tomatoes. For even more appeal, grow them in different colors, sizes, and shapes. Small pear-shaped yellow tomatoes are very pretty, and children like the mildly sweet flavor.

PAINLESS PROMPTING

OK, OK, I got the point, you say. But how, exactly, can I encourage my kids to eat more vegetables without being overbearing about it?

QUICK 🔲 *PAINLESS*

Fill a celery stick with a bit of peanut butter, then have your child arrange raisins in a line on top of the peanut butter. Voilà— "ants on a log."

- Serve the veggies first. Put them on the table just before you get ready to serve the meat or other main course. Your kids are usually pretty hungry at that point, and less likely to be picky. I sometimes put out raw carrot sticks, cucumber slices, or cut-up peppers as I'm finishing up dinner and the kids are asking, "When do we eat?" It's harder for them to nag when they're busy chewing.

- Make them pretty. I've always thought one of the reasons so many kids like broccoli and hate cabbage, even though the two vegetables aren't that differ-ent in flavor (or stink factor), is that broccoli is cute. It looks like trees.

- Serve them raw, or very lightly cooked. Kids like bright colors and crunchy textures, and often loathe slippery or mushy textures and strong-smelling foods. Caution: Be careful about serving hard raw vegetables (like carrots) in chunks to kids under the age of 4. If they don't know enough to chew them carefully, they could choke on them. (See Chapter 10, "Smooth Sailing—No More Mealtime Mutiny," for more on this.)

IF YOU'RE SO
INCLINED

Health food they're not, but maraschino cherries add pizzazz that kids can't resist. One mom said her finicky kids devoured cut-up pineapple and honeydew when she arranged them on a plate, spritzed on a bit of whipped topping, and topped the lot with a maraschino cherry.

Serve them often. One way I make sure the kids get enough fruits and vegetables is to try to serve at least one fruit or vegetable (preferably one that's not fried), at every meal. On a really lazy day, I may crack open a box of macaroni and cheese, but I serve it with sliced tomatoes, cut-up sweet peppers or apples, carrot sticks, or even just a glass of orange juice.

Play with them. Serve orange sections in half an orange shell. Freeze bananas on sticks for bananasicles. Spread cream cheese or peanut butter on bagels and let the kids make "faces" with raisins, cucumbers, carrots, or whatever else you have on hand. One friend of ours squeezes ranch dressing onto a plate in the shape of a bunny, then fans out carrot sticks as "whiskers." Hey, whatever works…

Serve them in a different form. If your fastidious kid doesn't like melon juice running down his chin, cut the cantaloupe into chunks. If a shredded carrot salad doesn't appeal, maybe carrot sticks will. If sliced tomatoes seem too "squishy," maybe cherry tomatoes will do the trick.

Hide them. Your kid may hate onions, but he probably won't notice them if they're chopped up and cooked in spaghetti sauce. Note: This does not work with all children. Some kids were born to eat with tweezers.

THE BEST AND WORST OF VEGGIES

So which commonly served vegetables do kids love, and which do they loathe? To find out, I conducted a highly unscientific survey of more than a dozen kids. The results:

Thumbs Up

Most of the kids gave these veggies a "yum" or "OK":

- Corn
- Potatoes
- Broccoli
- Raw carrots
- Cucumbers
- Lettuce
- Baked beans
- Regular beans (in chili and stuff like that)
- Green beans
- Peas
- Raw tomatoes
- Raw peppers (red and green)
- Onions (as long as they're cooked in sauces and such)

Mixed Reviews

The kids were fairly evenly divided over whether these were disgusting or good:

- Acorn squash
- Asparagus

QUICK 🞑 PAINLESS

To Easily Cut a Melon into Chunks:

1. Cut it into thin wedges.

2. Slide a knife between the flesh and the peel.

3. Slice through the melon at 1-inch intervals. (If the melon wedge is thick, make a second lengthwise or crosswise cut first.)

IF YOU'RE SO
INCLINED

Your daughter will only eat potatoes, bananas, carrots, and orange juice? Don't worry about it. Keep serving the other stuff, and one of these days she may try it.

- Beets
- Cauliflower
- Cooked carrots
- Mushrooms
- Garbanzos (chick-peas)
- Garlic (in sauces)
- Raw celery (several kids liked it only with peanut butter)
- Cooked spinach (most of the kids hadn't tried it raw)
- Cooked tomatoes (disgusting alone, but OK in sauces)
- Refried beans
- Sweet potatoes
- Olives (green and black)

Oh, Yuck!

Most of the kids hated these:

- Brussels sprouts
- Eggplant
- Cabbage (some like it in coleslaw)
- Cooked peppers (red or green)
- Zucchini
- Cooked celery (those that said they'd tried it)

Colorful Veggie Stir-Fry

Stir-frying the vege-tables one at a time helps keep their flavors separate.

- **Preparation Time:** 5 minutes
- **Cooking Time:** 7 to 8 minutes
- **Servings:** 4

2 tablespoons canola or vegetable oil

1 tablespoon minced garlic

2 teaspoons minced ginger

1 cup chopped green onions (optional)

2 tablespoons water

2 cups miniature corn, drained

1 cup sliced red or green peppers

1 cup sliced fresh mushrooms (optional)

6 ounces (1 bag) washed and trimmed fresh spinach

1 cup diced, cooked chicken or pork, or firm tofu, cubed

$^1/_3$ cup bottled light (reduced-sodium) stir-fry sauce

1. Heat the oil in a wok or in a deep, nonstick frying pan over medium-high heat. Add the garlic, ginger, and green onions and cook, tossing and stirring, for just a few seconds, until you can smell the garlic.

2. Add the remaining vegetables, one at a time, stir-frying each one for a minute before adding the next vegetable. Gently stir in the chicken, pork, or tofu and the sauce. Cook for another minute, or just until heated through.

3. Serve hot over cooked rice or noodles.

IF YOU'RE SO INCLINED

Tofu works best in stir-fries if you squeeze out the excess liquid first. To do this, cut the tofu into slices, then put it between layers of paper towels. Press gently but firmly.

Baked Potatoes Topped with Roasted Vegetables

Roasted vegetables, a fairly new entry in the frozen food aisle, cook up into a luscious "stew." If your kids don't go for them, top the potatoes with something else. Try leftover spaghetti sauce, chili, or beef stew; chopped cooked chicken with salsa; or even baked beans.

- **Preparation Time:** 5 minutes
- **Baking Time:** 40 to 50 minutes
- **Servings:** 6

6 medium to large baking potatoes, washed and pricked several times with a paring knife

One 1-pound, 10-ounce package frozen roasted vegetables

2 tablespoons olive oil

$^1/_2$ to $^3/_4$ cup grated part-skim mozzarella cheese, to taste

1 Preheat the oven to 425°F. Set the potatoes directly on the top oven rack. Bake for about 50 minutes, or until the potatoes can be easily pierced with a fork.

2 While the potatoes are baking, prepare the vegetables. Spread the oil in the bottom of an ovenproof casserole. Add the vegetables, mixing them with the oil. Bake, uncovered, for 20 minutes, or until heated through.

YOU'LL THANK YOURSELF LATER

When you cook baking potatoes in the microwave, put them on a paper towel. This helps absorb moisture and makes them come out fluffier, like genuine baked potatoes.

3 Remove the potatoes from the oven, using potholders. Set the potatoes aside for a couple of minutes. Cut them lengthwise and squeeze the bottom of the potatoes to fan them open. Top with the warm vegetables and sprinkle with the cheese. Serve immediately.

Variation: If you're in a rush, you can cook the potatoes and vegetables in the microwave. Cook the potatoes on high (100 percent) for 10 to 15 minutes, then cook the vegetable topping for 5 to 7 minutes. It's actually easier, though, to use the oven. And the vegetables taste better baked.

QUICK 🔘 PAINLESS

Kids don't like the seasoning blend that comes with the frozen vegetables? Just omit it—or substitute your family's favorite herb or spice.

Mediterranean Couscous

Again, here's a recipe with adjustable ingredients. Omit the olives if you don't like them. Add some red onions if you're partial to them. Substitute grated fresh Parmesan for the feta cheese.

- **Preparation Time:** 5 to 10 minutes
- **Cooking Time:** 5 minutes
- **Servings:** 6 (as a side dish or salad)

$2^1/_4$ cups water or chicken broth

$1^1/_2$ cups couscous

8 to 10 cherry tomatoes, washed

Pitted black olives, preferably Greek

$^1/_3$ cup crumbled feta cheese

$^1/_2$ to 1 cup sliced cucumbers

1 tablespoon red wine vinegar, or 2 tablespoons Italian salad dressing

Salt and pepper to taste

1. Put the water or chicken broth in a saucepan and bring it to a boil. Stir in the couscous, cover with a tight lid, and remove the pan from the heat. Let the couscous stand for 5 minutes. Uncover, and fluff it with a fork to separate the grains.

2. Toss the couscous with the tomatoes, olives, cheese, cucumbers, vinegar or salad dressing, and salt and pepper. Serve warm or at room temperature.

QUICK ⬤ PAINLESS

Couscous (koos-koos), or "baby pasta," is a busy parents' best friend. You don't even have to cook it—just steep it in boiling liquid. It goes with anything pasta does. Serve it for dinner with savory toppings or for breakfast with fruit.

Warm Fruit Medley

Barbara Grunes, who contributed this and most of the other recipes in the book, said this was a childhood favorite. It's designed to use up ripe fruit that's starting to go soft. You can make it with almost any fruit.

- **Preparation Time:** 5 to 10 minutes
- **Cooking Time:** 6 to 8 minutes
- **Servings:** 6

2 bananas, peeled and sliced

1 cup raspberries, washed

2 apples, peeled, cored and sliced

2 mangos or 3 peaches, peeled, pitted, and sliced

3 pears, peeled, cored and sliced

$^1/_4$ cup sugar, or to taste

1 teaspoon ground cinnamon

3 tablespoons water or orange juice

1 Put the prepared fruit in a saucepan with the sugar, cinnamon, and water or juice. Simmer for 5 to 8 minutes, stirring occasionally. The fruit will blend together.

2 Spoon the warm fruit over buttered noodles, rice, couscous, pancakes, or waffles. Add a scoop of creamed cottage cheese, ricotta cheese, or yogurt for a complete meal.

YOU'LL THANK YOURSELF LATER

Always cook fruit and other acidic foods in stainless steel, enameled, or anodized aluminum pans. Cooking them in plain aluminum or cast-iron pans can discolor the pans and create "off" flavors in the food.

Sweet Potatoes with Turkey Sloppy Joe

Preparation Time: 5 minutes

Cooking Time: 10 minutes (for the topping)

Servings: 6

6 medium sweet potatoes, scrubbed

1 pound lean ground turkey

$^1/_2$ cup finely chopped onion

1 cup chopped celery

$^1/_2$ cup finely chopped green bell pepper

1 cup of your family's favorite barbecue sauce

Salt and pepper to taste

1. Set the sweet potatoes, thick ends pointing out, in a circle on a paper towel in the microwave. Cook on high (100 percent) for 8 to 12 minutes, or until they can be easily pierced with a fork. (The sweet potatoes also can be baked in a preheated 425°F oven for 1 hour.)

2. While the sweet potatoes are cooking, prepare the sloppy joe sauce. Cook the turkey in a large nonstick frying pan over medium heat for 3 to 4 minutes. Stir in the onion, celery, and pepper. Continue cooking until the turkey is no longer pink, stirring occasionally. Mix in the barbecue sauce. Bring the mixture to a boil, then remove from the heat.

3. Remove the sweet potatoes to plates, using potholders. Cut open each potato lengthwise and squeeze the bottom to open up the potato. Set a potato on each plate. Spoon some of the sauce on the top of each potato and serve hot.

QUICK 🔲 PAINLESS

Ground turkey can be high in fat, if it includes the skin. Look for labels that say "extra-lean ground turkey breast."

Kids' Favorite Broccoli Salad

Buy the broccoli already cut up and the carrots already grated (in the supermarket produce department, salad bar, or deli), and this salad goes together just like that.

Preparation Time: 5 minutes

Servings: 4 to 6

4 cups broccoli florets

$^1/_2$ cup grated carrots, or carrot-raisin salad

$^1/_4$ cup raisins

$^1/_4$ cup chopped red onion (optional)

$^1/_4$ cup roasted sunflower seed kernels

Dressing:

5 tablespoons orange juice

5 tablespoons light mayonnaise

2 to 3 teaspoons sugar, to taste

1 Mix the broccoli, carrots, raisins, onion, and sunflower seeds in a bowl.

2 Mix together the orange juice, mayonnaise, and sugar. Add to the salad and toss to coat the vegetables with the dressing. Chill until serving time.

So your kids ate all their vegetables without complaining? Let them do something a bit out of the norm: stay up late, bang on the set of drums Uncle Alex sent them, sleep in sleeping bags instead of their beds.

The Lazy Way

Getting Time on Your Side

	The Old Way	The Lazy Way
Getting Junior to eat peas	1 hour	0 hours
Cutting up melon	15 minutes	5 minutes
Preparing veggies for stir-fry	30 minutes	10 minutes
Making Mediterranean pasta	15 minutes	5 minutes
Cooking sweet potatoes	1 hour	10 minutes
Making broccoli salad	15 minutes	5 minutes

Quicker by the Pot

Our great-grandmas always had big pots of stuff simmering on the stove. And no wonder: They had 6, or 8, or 10 kids and a nonstop schedule of cooking and housework.

Although today's families tend to be a lot smaller, things really haven't changed all that much. Today, we're all busy following different pursuits, so the strategy of cooking one big pot of food for two or three meals still makes sense. If you make a big pot of soup on Sunday, you've already taken care of Monday night's dinner.

Does this mean I think you should spend all weekend baking bread and cooking up huge pots of soup and spaghetti sauce? No way! I don't know about you, but I usually have better things to do with my weekend, even if it's something exciting like pulling weeds or catching up on the kids' dental visits.

None of the dishes that follow, except for the baked beans, takes very long to cook. And the beans bake without requiring attention, so you can go pick up your son from school while they're in the oven.

If you are into making a lot of stews and slow-cooked dishes, you might want to invest in a pressure cooker or a crockpot (slow cooker). Both give you a lazy way to make stews, soups, and sauces.

THE RECIPES

If you have three or four people in your family, all of these dishes will make two full meals. If your family is larger or your appetites bigger, you should still get at least enough leftovers for somebody's lunch the next day.

Vegetable Soup

Add whatever vegetables and meats you like to the tomato-broth base to adapt this soup to your family's tastes. You can also make a "cream" soup by pureeing half the soup in a blender.

Preparation Time: 6 to 10 minutes

Cooking Time: 40 minutes

Servings: 8 to 10

1 tablespoon canola or olive oil
1 cup chopped defrosted onions
One 48-ounce can chicken broth
One 28-ounce can crushed tomatoes, with liquid
1 cup sliced or diced celery
1 cup sliced, diced, or shredded carrots
One 10-ounce package frozen string beans, defrosted
1 cup leftover cooked potatoes or frozen hash browns
Pepper and dried basil to taste
1 or 2 cups diced cooked chicken or turkey breast, optional

QUICK **n** *PAINLESS*

Grandma roasted a chicken every Sunday, but her granddaughter buys roasted chicken from the supermarket. Dress up rotisserie chicken by sprinkling it with herbs or drizzling it with barbecue sauce. Round out the dinner with mashed potatoes and corn (from the freezer, of course) and refrigerator biscuits, or with deli salads.

1 Heat the oil in a large saucepan or a soup pot over medium heat. Add the onions and cook, stirring occasionally, for 5 minutes, or until softened.

2 Stir in the chicken broth and crushed tomatoes.

3 Add the celery and carrots, and stir to combine. Bring the soup to a boil, then reduce the heat to a simmer. Partially cover and continue cooking for 25 minutes.

4 Add the beans, potatoes, and chicken or turkey, and season with pepper and basil. Continue cooking for 5 minutes, just to heat through the ingredients.

Variation: Make the tomato-broth base, then add to it: 2 cups sliced fresh mushrooms; one 10-ounce package frozen chopped broccoli; one 10-ounce package frozen peas; 2 or 3 corn tortillas, cut into strips with scissors; 1 cup cooked rice or pasta, and 1 cup diced lean ham or cooked pork.

YOU'LL THANK YOURSELF LATER

When the soup has cooled a bit, ladle it into pint-size freezer-to-microwave containers in single-serving portions. Then you, your spouse, or your kids can quickly reheat it in the microwave.

Arizona-Style Rice and Bean Casserole

This is one of those "stir and cook" dishes that come in so handy for weeknight meals. Not only is it quick, but it makes enough leftovers for tomorrow's lunch or even dinner. Serve it with plenty of baked corn chips and a green salad.

- **Preparation Time:** 5 to 10 minutes
- **Baking Time:** 15 to 20 minutes in the oven; 7 to 8 minutes in the microwave
- **Servings:** 6 to 8

1 tablespoon canola or olive oil

1 cup chopped onions

2 teaspoons minced garlic (optional)

4 cups cooked rice

One 10-ounce package frozen corn kernels

One 15-ounce can kidney or pinto beans, drained

1 cup nonfat or low-fat, small-curd cottage cheese

One 4^1/$_2$-ounce can peeled and chopped green chiles, drained

2 teaspoons chili powder

1 teaspoon prepared mustard

Salt and pepper

8 ounces grated reduced-fat sharp Cheddar cheese (optional)

IF YOU'RE SO INCLINED

Rather than serving corn chips on the side, you can layer the bean and cheese mixture with 4 to 6 corn tortillas in the casserole dish. Bake, rather than microwave, the layered casserole.

1 You can make this either in the oven or in the microwave. If using the oven, preheat it to 375°F.

2 Heat the oil in a nonstick frying pan. Add the onions and garlic and cook over medium heat for a few minutes, stirring occasionally, until softened.

3 Place the rice, corn, beans, cottage cheese, chiles, and seasonings in a 2-quart microwave- or ovenproof covered casserole. Add the onions and garlic and mix everything together. Top with the cheddar cheese if desired.

4 Microwave on high (100 percent) for 7 to 8 minutes, stirring twice, until heated through. Or cover and bake for 15 to 20 minutes, until heated through.

5 Serve hot in bowls, with corn chips.

QUICK n PAINLESS

If you need a dessert in a hurry and your freezer is bare, stick a container or two of nonfat vanilla or lemon yogurt in the freezer. Freeze until solid. Let it soften at room temperature for 5 to 10 minutes before serving.

Salsa-Spiked Spaghetti Sauce

For a truly "lazy way" to top pasta, just open a jar of pre-pared pasta sauce. You'll find some very good ones in the supermarket. One friend likes to keep canned clams on hand as well; she mixes them with bottled pasta sauce for an instant clam sauce.

However, there's still something very satisfying about home-made sauce, and it's easy enough to make.

This recipe makes enough sauce for two meals. You also can double the recipe and freeze the rest for a "rainy day."

- **Preparation Time:** 15 minutes
- **Cooking Time:** 35 to 40 minutes
- **Servings:** 8 servings

2 tablespoons olive oil or olive oil nonstick cooking spray

1 cup chopped onions

1 tablespoon minced garlic

1 cup chopped red or green peppers, or grated or finely chopped carrots

1 pound ground turkey or very lean ground beef

One 28-ounce can crushed tomatoes, including juice

One 6-ounce can tomato paste

1 teaspoon honey

One 11-ounce jar bottled chunky salsa (mild or medium)

2 teaspoons dried basil

1 teaspoon dried oregano

Salt and pepper

IF YOU'RE SO INCLINED

Spaghetti sauce isn't just for spaghetti. Try it spooned over polenta, couscous, rice, baked potatoes—even toast, if you're really in a hurry.

1 Heat the oil in a large saucepan over medium heat.

2 Add the onions, garlic, and peppers or carrots, and cook for a few minutes, until the onions soften.

3 Add the turkey and cook until the meat is no longer pink, stirring occasionally. Drain off any fat.

4 Stir in the crushed tomatoes and juice, tomato paste, honey, salsa, and spices.

5 Bring the sauce to a boil. Reduce the heat and simmer for 25 to 30 minutes, stirring occasionally.

6 Arrange hot, cooked pasta on individual plates and ladle the sauce over the top. Serve with grated fresh Parmesan or Romano cheese.

YOU'LL THANK YOURSELF LATER

Cook up a double batch of pasta to go with this sauce. The next evening, put the leftover pasta in a colander and run it under hot running water to warm it. Or, if you have only a handful of leftover noodles, toss them in with a new batch of pasta as it's boiling, just before you're ready to drain it.

Dad's Baked Beans

Sure, you can just open a can or two of baked beans and heat 'em up—in fact, I highly recommend that when you're in a real hurry to get dinner on the table. But they just don't have that nice slow-baked texture or flavor.

My husband's the baked-bean cook in the family. He's tried cooking the beans from scratch, but it can be a frustrating process (especially because we live at 5,000 feet). So he starts with plain Michigan-grown Great Northern beans in jars, then flavors and bakes them.

If you have a slow cooker or pressure cooker, you can try cooking the dried Great Northern beans from scratch.

Serve these with plenty of bread.

- **Preparation Time:** 5 minutes
- **Baking Time:** 3 hours
- **Servings:** 8 to 10

Three 15-ounce cans or one 48-ounce jar Great Northern beans

3 tablespoons molasses, or to taste

2 to 4 tablespoons brown sugar (use the lesser amount if the barbecue sauce is very sweet)

2 teaspoons dry mustard

$^3/_4$ cup of your favorite barbecue sauce

1 onion, cut in wedges (optional)

$^1/_2$ to 1 cup cooked, diced or crumbled meat (such as left-over hamburger, pork roast, or ham); optional

You've cooked four nights this week. Now put your feet up and let your fingers walk to the phone listing for the nearest eatery that delivers.

The Lazy Way

1. Preheat the oven to 300°F. Oil or spray a glass or clay casserole dish, or a glass 9-by-13-inch pan.

2. Pour the beans and their liquid into the casserole dish. Stir in the molasses, brown sugar, mustard, and barbecue sauce, making sure they're distributed through the beans.

3. Place the onion wedges here and there in the beans. Do the same with the meat, if you're using it.

4. Cover the dish and bake the beans in the center of the oven for 2 hours. Uncover, and bake another 30 minutes, or until the beans have thickened and have a nice crust on the top.

5. Serve hot or cold.

A COMPLETE WASTE OF TIME

The 3 Worst Things to Do with Beans:

1. Add acid when you're cooking dried beans from scratch. It toughens the skins.

2. Add baking soda to the water. It destroys nutrients.

3. Overcook them or undercook them. They should be tender but not mushy.

IF YOU'RE SO
INCLINED

Like most chilis, this one taste even better the next day. For a heartier meal, cook up some spaghetti, rice, cornbread, or baked potatoes, and spoon the leftover chili over them.

Four-Bean Chili

With this recipe you can "feed them veggies without them knowing it." It is loaded with folate (the beans); vitamin A, (the carrots); and vitamin C (the tomatoes).

- **Preparation Time:** 5 to 10 minutes
- **Cooking Time:** 25 minutes
- **Servings:** 8

2 tablespoons olive or canola oil

1 cup chopped onions

2 tablespoons minced garlic

Two 15-ounce cans kidney or pinto beans, drained

Two 15-ounce cans black beans, drained

One 15-ounce can garbanzos (chick-peas), drained

1 cup grated carrots

One 28-ounce can crushed tomatoes, including juice

One 14^1/$_2$-ounce can green (string) beans

3 tablespoons chili powder

1 tablespoon ground cumin

Salt and pepper to taste

1 Heat the oil in a large, heavy pot or Dutch oven. Add the onions and garlic and cook a few minutes, stirring occasionally, until the onions soften. Add the remaining ingredients and mix to combine.

2 Cook, uncovered, over medium-low heat, stirring occasionally, for 20 minutes. The chili will thicken slightly as it cooks.

3 Taste, and adjust the seasonings as necessary. Serve hot, with crackers, baked corn chips, or corn bread.

Getting Time on Your Side

	The Old Way	The Lazy Way
Chopping vegetables for soup	20 minutes	Buy them chopped
Making frozen yogurt	$2\frac{1}{2}$ hours	2 hours
Making homemade baked beans	6 hours	3 hours
Cooking pasta	15 minutes	2 minutes
Cooking a casserole	45 minutes	5 to 15 minutes
Preparing tomorrow night's dinner	30 minutes	It's already done

Creative Cheating

In the 1950s, as women grew increasingly liberated from the stove, recipes using convenience foods, such as canned soup, came into vogue. Such casseroles have never really gone out of fashion with most folks, for the simple reason that they're satisfying and easy to make. Let's face it, this is "Mom's comfort food" at its most basic (though Dad can certainly make it, too).

I confess that plenty of my weekday meals involve opening boxes, bags, and cans, especially in the winter when the fresh produce is often less than inspiring. The supermarket is a horn of plenty when it comes to ready-made foods. With a little sleight of hand, you can dress them up so they no longer are just plain old tomato soup, but Mom or Dad's extra-special tomato soup. Or noodle casserole. Or pot roast.

THE RECIPES

Here's a collection of dishes that start with packaged mixes or other convenience foods, but are much more special than the sum of their parts. As a bonus, many of these are things that kids (or fumble-fingered spouses) can help with.

Double Blueberry Muffins

Muffins made from scratch are easy, but muffins from a mix are even easier. The extra blueberries and the crunchy topping lift these muffins out of the ordinary.

- **Preparation Time:** 10 minutes
- **Baking Time:** 20 minutes
- **Servings:** Makes 12 muffins

One 7-ounce package blueberry muffin mix (and the ingredients required on package directions)

1 cup fresh or defrosted blueberries

$^1/_2$ to $^3/_4$ cup quick (not instant) rolled oats

$^1/_2$ cup sugar

1$^1/_2$ tablespoons butter or margarine, at room temperature

1. Preheat the oven to 400°F. Line a 12-cup muffin tin with paper cupcake liners.

2. Prepare the muffin mix according to the package directions. Mix in the drained blueberries that come with the mix, then gently stir in the extra blueberries. Spoon the batter into the muffin cups.

3. In a small bowl, mix the oats, sugar, and butter together with a fork or with your fingertips. Sprinkle this mixture on the muffins.

4. Bake in the center of the oven for 20 minutes (or the time recommended on the muffin mix package), or until the muffins are firm.

5. Remove the muffins from the pan and sit them on a wire rack to cool. Serve warm or at room temperature.

YOU'LL THANK YOURSELF LATER

Freeze half of the muffins for brown-bag lunches or quick breakfasts. Put a frozen muffin directly in the lunchbox; it'll be thawed by lunchtime. To defrost or reheat a muffin for breakfast, microwave it on medium for 30 seconds to 1 minute.

Chicken or Tuna Noodle Casserole

This comforting dish is even more convenient when you buy the vegetables ready-chopped. Serve it with a tossed green salad—from a bag, of course.

Preparation Time: 5 to 10 minutes

Cooking Time: 35 minutes

Servings: 6

12 ounces spaghetti or fettuccini, cooked according to package directions

2 tablespoons butter or margarine, at room temperature

1 cup sliced or chopped celery, or frozen peas

1 cup sliced or chopped red or green peppers, or sliced fresh mushrooms, or frozen, defrosted green beans

$^1/_2$ cup chopped onions

One $10^3/_4$-ounce can condensed cream of chicken soup (preferably the reduced-fat, reduced-sodium kind)

1 cup 2 percent milk

4 to 6 ounces grated reduced-fat sharp Cheddar cheese

1 tablespoon Worcestershire sauce

$^1/_4$ teaspoon salt

$^1/_2$ teaspoon white pepper

$1^1/_2$ to $1^3/_4$ cups diced cooked skinless chicken or turkey, or two 6-ounce cans water-packed tuna, drained

1 Preheat the oven to 350°F. Lightly oil or spray an oven-proof casserole or 9-by-13-inch glass baking dish.

2 Mix all of the ingredients in the baking dish. (If the noodles have been refrigerated, run them under hot water first.)

3 Bake for 35 minutes, or until heated through. Serve.

QUICK ⊞ PAINLESS

Noodle casserole is an easy way to use up left-over turkey from Thanksgiving. You can even sprinkle some of the leftover stuffing over the noodles to make a crusty topping.

Tomato-Spinach Soup

This soup makes a good winter main course, served with a salad and plenty of bread. Leftovers are good heated up the next day for lunch.

The soup will taste richer and curdle a bit less if made with reduced-fat (2 percent) milk.

Preparation Time: 10 minutes

Cooking Time: 8 to 10 minutes

Servings: 8

2 tablespoons canola or olive oil
1 cup chopped onions
Three $10^3/_4$-ounce cans condensed cream of tomato soup
3 cups nonfat or reduced-fat (2 percent) milk
One 12-ounce package frozen chopped spinach, defrosted
Pepper and dried dill weed (or basil), to taste

1. Heat the oil in a large saucepan over medium heat. Add the onions and cook a few minutes, stirring occasionally, until softened.

2. Stir in the tomato soup, milk, and spinach. Stir to combine. Bring the soup to a boil, then reduce the heat to a simmer and continue cooking for 5 to 7 minutes, until the soup and spinach are heated through.

3. Serve the soup in a bowl, by itself or over cooked rice or noodles.

IF YOU'RE SO INCLINED

This soup is even tastier made with fresh chopped basil or dill. If it's summer, you also can stir in a chopped raw tomato before serving.

Tomato-Corn Soup

This variation is good in the summer. With the pieces of corn in it, it's a messy dish—which of course appeals to kids. If the mess factor is a bit too much for you, cut the corn kernels off the cob, or use canned or frozen corn.

- **Preparation Time:** 10 minutes
- **Cooking Time:** 5 to 7 minutes
- **Servings:** 8

3 ears fresh corn on the cob, or two 10-ounce packages frozen corn on the cob in pieces

2 tablespoons canola or olive oil

1 cup chopped onions

Three $10^3/_4$-ounce condensed cream of tomato soup

3 cups nonfat or reduced-fat (2 percent) milk

Salt and pepper to taste

3 cups air-popped popcorn for garnish (optional)

1 If using fresh corn, husk it (or better, have the kids husk it), remove the stalk, and cut each ear into 3 pieces. If using frozen corn, get the kind that's cut in pieces.

2 Heat the oil in a large saucepan over medium heat. Add the onions and cook a few minutes, stirring occasionally, or until softened.

3 Stir in the tomato soup, milk, and the corn pieces. Bring the soup to a boil. Reduce the heat to a simmer and continue cooking for 5 to 7 minutes, or until the soup and corn are heated through. Ladle the soup into bowls and float the popped corn on top. Serve hot.

QUICK ⬛ PAINLESS

For an even "cornier" dinner, buy some cornbread or corn muffins to go along with the Tomato-Corn Soup.

Beef Stew with a Cornbread "Hat"

This dish takes a while to cook, but requires very little actual hands-on preparation. And it's worth the wait. Nothing hits the spot on a cold winter day better than a good stew. The vegetables in this one cook into a luscious gravy.

- **Preparation Time:** About 5 to 10 minutes
- **Cooking Time:** 1½ hours
- **Servings:** 6

2 tablespoons canola or olive oil

1 cup chopped onions

2 teaspoons minced garlic

1³/₄ to 2 pounds boneless beef stew meat (or buy a chuck roast and have the butcher cut it into stew-size pieces)

2 tablespoons flour or cornstarch

One 1-pound 10-ounce package frozen roasted vegetables, including seasoning packet

1 teaspoon celery salt

¹/₂ teaspoon pepper

³/₄ cup water

One 8¹/₂-ounce package cornbread mix

1 egg white

¹/₃ cup nonfat milk

1. Heat the oil in a Dutch oven or other large, ovenproof saucepan. Stir in the onions and garlic.

2. Sprinkle the meat with the flour and add it to the pot. Add the vegetables, seasoning packet, celery salt, and pepper. Stir in the water.

QUICK 🞙 PAINLESS

If you prefer your corn-bread a little richer, use a whole egg and/or whole milk instead of an egg white and nonfat milk.

3. Cover and simmer over medium-low heat for 1 hour. Stir the stew occasionally and add more water if necessary.

4. Preheat the oven to 400°F.

5. Prepare the cornbread mix according to the package directions, using the egg white and nonfat milk. Do not overbeat.

6. Remove the lid of the pot and spread the cornbread batter over the top of the stew.

7. Using pot holders, transfer the pot, uncovered, to the center of the oven, and bake for 20 minutes or until the cornbread is done.

8. Spoon the stew onto plates, including some of the cornbread "hat" with each serving. Serve hot.

IF YOU'RE SO

INCLINED

Beef stew doesn't have to be just for the kids; it's good enough for company. "Beef it up" for adults by adding sophisticated vegetables such as sliced portobello mushrooms or frozen, defrosted artichoke hearts.

Invite the kids into the kitchen. While the breadsticks are still warm, take turns dipping them into a bit of honey. Yum.

The Lazy Way

Seed Breadsticks

If you don't have a bread machine, frozen bread dough is the next best thing. If you do have a bread machine, make 1 pound of the dough on page 189 and use it in this recipe.

- **Preparation Time:** 10 to 15 minutes (not including dough defrosting times)
- **Baking Time:** 20 to 25 minutes
- **Servings:** 8

$^1/_4$ cup margarine or butter

1 loaf (1 pound) frozen bread dough, preferably whole wheat, defrosted according to package directions

2 tablespoons sesame seeds

2 tablespoons poppy seeds

2 tablespoons caraway seeds (or additional sesame or poppy seeds)

1. Preheat the oven to 375°F.

2. Put the margarine or butter in a small microwave-proof container. Microwave on high (100 percent) for 30 seconds, until melted. Set aside.

3. Divide the bread into 8 equal portions. Using clean hands, roll out each dough piece into a pencil shape about 8 inches long. Brush the breadsticks with the melted margarine or butter.

4. Combine the seeds on a paper plate. Roll the bread sticks in the seeds. Set the breadsticks on a nonstick cookie sheet.

5. Bake in the center of the oven for 20 to 25 minutes, or until golden and firm. Cool the breadsticks on a wire rack.

Getting Time on Your Side

	The Old Way	The Lazy Way
Roasting the Sunday chicken	2 hours	0 hours
Making muffins	20 minutes	10 minutes
Cutting up vegetables for stew	15 minutes	0 minutes
Making "homemade" tomato soup	40 minutes	8 minutes
Mixing dough for breadsticks	30 minutes	0 minutes
Making cornbread	15 minutes	5 minutes

Let Them Beat Cake

Food is not just about fuel. It's about nurturing and family traditions and love.

Unfortunately (in my opinion, anyway), cooking is now viewed as a sport, like bungee-jumping, an activity that may be fun but is in no way an essential part of life. Cruise the Internet, and the search engines list cooking and food under "Entertainment and Leisure."

On a practical level, of course, you really don't have to cook, and busy parents have all kinds of excellent ready-prepared foods to rely on these days. You can easily live on carryout, restaurant food, and supermarket fare.

So why on earth should you teach your kids to cook? There are a number of reasons:

It's a Way to Save Money

Maybe you can afford carryout all the time, but at some point your child will probably be in his first job, struggling to make rent and car payments. Eating high-quality, nutritious carry-out and restaurant food gets awfully expensive, and eating cheap "junk food" is rarely the path to good nutrition.

If you garden, stake out a small plot for the kids. Gardening helps teach them responsibility, and they're more likely to eat vegetables they've grown themselves. Lettuce, spinach, radishes, and carrots are easy to grow and don't take up much space.

It's a Way to Pass On the Family Heritage and Traditions

Do you want your great aunt's wonderful sweet potato pie to die with you? Food ties into holidays, ethnic background, and religious tradition. There are a lot of turkey stuffings out there, but the one I make every year is a variation on my mom's. Thanksgiving wouldn't be the same without it.

Food traditions can be as simple as having roast chicken every Sunday, or making potato pancakes just the way your family likes them, or picking apples as a family every October, or sending a tin of dried fruit every Christmas to friends and relatives.

It's a Way to Get Home-Cooked Food Without Having to Make It Yourself

What if your kid *likes* to cook? Just think—a captive chef. My mom has never cared much for cooking, so she was more than happy to let me in the kitchen when I got interested. I've been cooking for the family (if only off and on) ever since.

WHAT CAN THE KIDS DO IN THE KITCHEN?

Kids should be assigned food preparation and cooking tasks appropriate to their ages. That way, they stay safe and keep from getting overly frustrated.

Ages 2 to 3

- Stir foods, with some help from Mom and Dad

- Push the button on a bread machine (Keep it out of their reach when it's not in use, so they won't think this is a fun new game.)

- Decorate cookies and cakes with sprinkles, as long as you're not fussy about the results or the mess

Ages 4 to 6

- Make their own sandwiches, without cutting them

- Measure foods, with help

- Stir foods

- 6-year-olds often can peel carrots with a vegetable peeler, with supervision

- Knead and shape bread dough, if you're not too precise about the results

- Load dishes in the dishwasher

- Cut out and decorate cookies

- Help arrange the toppings on pizza

Ages 7 to 10

- Use bread knives (at ages 6 to 7) and sharper knives (ages 9 to 10) to cut foods, with supervision

- Wash dishes by hand, with some supervision

- Accurately measure foods

- Frost cakes and cookies

- Shape foods (such as bread dough) fairly accurately

- Peel carrots and maybe potatoes

QUICK **IP** PAINLESS

A plastic 1-cup liquid measure is ideal for small children to practice with. They can easily lift the lightweight cup, and it won't break if they drop it.

YOU'LL THANK YOURSELF LATER

Get your fledgling chef his own cookbook. Kids love recipes tailored just for them. You can also find just-for-kids recipes on the Internet.

- Measure out the ingredients and make bread in the machine
- Use a microwave or toaster oven, with supervision
- 9- and 10-year-olds can begin to use the stove or oven, with close supervision

Ages 10 to 12
- Bake and cook simple dishes, with some help (for example, you need to drain boiling pasta)
- Pick up a couple of items at the neighborhood market (basic personal safety rules apply)
- Help you grocery shop and plan menus
- Follow recipes with less supervision

Ages 13 on Up
- Plan menus and cook meals for themselves and the family
- Grocery shop, with detailed instructions
- Handle more sophisticated tasks (for example, adapting recipes to their tastes)
- Use the stove, oven, and appliances with minimal supervision (ages 13 to 14) and no supervision (15+)

THE RECIPES

You'll notice there are several bread recipes in this chapter. That's no accident. Kids love to play with bread dough. It's bouncy and can be molded into different shapes. They also can make it in a breadmaker. Even a toddler can push the button or pour in a cup of water.

Basic Bread

This basic dough works well for any of the bread recipes in this book.

- **Preparation Time:** 5 minutes
- **Kneading, Rising, and Baking Times:** Depends on machine
- **Servings:** 12 to 14

$1^1/_4$ cups water

1 teaspoon salt

3 tablespoons honey

$^1/_2$ cup quick (not instant) oats

$^3/_4$ cup whole wheat flour

2 cups bread flour

3 teaspoons active dry yeast

1. Put all the ingredients in the bread pan, following the manufacturer's instructions.

2. Bake on the regular white bread setting. Or use the dough setting if you plan to shape the dough into something besides a regular loaf.

Variation: If you don't have a breadmaker, this recipe works fine the regular way. Mix the yeast with the water (the water should be warm), then mix in the other ingredients. Put the dough in an oiled bowl and let it rise until doubled, then punch it down (kids love to do this), shape as you like, let rise again, and bake at 375°F for 35 to 40 minutes for a regular loaf, 20 to 25 minutes for bread sticks, or 15 to 20 minutes for rolls. Makes a $1^1/_2$-pound loaf.

QUICK n' PAINLESS

If you run out of time (or energy), you can cover your bread dough and let it sit overnight in the refrigerator. Bring it to room temperature the next day, and let it rise.

Bean and Chicken Burritos

Kids over the age of 12 can make this entire dish. Younger children can help spread the filling on the tortillas and roll them up.

Preparation Time: 15 minutes

Cooking Time: 6 to 8 minutes

Servings: 4

One 16-ounce can fat-free refried beans
1 cup chopped cooked chicken, turkey, or lean ham—
    or use additional beans
2 teaspoons chili powder
3 tablespoons canned chopped green chiles, drained
    (or use chopped sweet peppers)
3 tablespoons chopped fresh cilantro (or parsley)
4 flour tortillas, preferably whole wheat
1 cup grated Monterey Jack or Cheddar cheese
One 16-ounce jar bottled salsa or 2 cups fresh salsa

1 Preheat the oven to 350°F.

2 In a bowl, mix together the beans, chicken, chili powder, chiles, and cilantro.

3 Lay each tortilla flat and spread about ¹/₃ cup filling down the center of the tortilla. Sprinkle with a tablespoon or two of the grated cheese.

QUICK ⟨ⁱⁱ⟩ PAINLESS

Young children often find it easier to use a small rubber spatula, or even the back of a small wooden spoon, to spread fillings such as refried beans or peanut butter. They don't have the dexterity yet to gracefully handle butter knives.

4 Roll up the tortilla, folding the top and bottom edges over the filling, and then fold in the sides. Set the burritos, seam side down, in an ovenproof pan or on a cookie sheet. Sprinkle the remaining cheese over the tops.

5 Bake the burritos about 6 to 8 minutes, or until the cheese melts. Place a burrito on each plate and spoon the salsa on top. Serve hot.

IF YOU'RE SO
INCLINED

When you sauté chicken breasts, cook 2 to 3 pounds' worth. Use some of the chicken for burritos, some in a stir-fry, and the rest for sandwiches.

Animal Pancakes

Young children can help stir the batter and choose the animal shapes they'd like, and older children can help cook the pancakes, with supervision. Bring a sturdy chair or stepstool next to the stove. Never let young children "cook" unattended at the stove.

Serve these with honey, jam, maple syrup, fruit syrup, or canned or fresh fruit.

For an even easier version, make the pancakes from a mix.

- **Preparation Time:** 20 minutes (including batter resting time)
- **Cooking Time:** 5 minutes
- **Servings:** 6

$1^1/_2$ cups all-purpose flour (you can substitute whole wheat flour for $^1/_2$ cup of the flour)

1 teaspoon baking powder

$^1/_2$ teaspoon salt

1 egg

$1^1/_4$ cups milk

1 tablespoon melted butter or margarine

Fresh blueberries, or a mashed banana (optional)

Butter-flavored cooking spray

1. In a mixing bowl, combine the flour, baking powder, and salt. Mix in the egg, milk, and butter.

2. Let the batter stand for 15 minutes (this is optional, but makes more tender pancakes), then stir. If you're using the mashed banana, add it to the batter now.

IF YOU'RE SO
INCLINED

Either you, or the child (with your help) can make a whole menagerie of pancakes. Snakes are easy for kids to make. Or make cats (round pancakes with pointed ears), fish (oval pancakes with a tail), or elephants (round pancakes with a long trunk). Use blueberries for "eyes" and "noses."

3 Coat a nonstick frying pan with the cooking spray, and heat it over medium heat. Drop the batter from a tablespoon into the pan, and either make round pancakes or animal shapes. If you're using blueberries, sprinkle them over the batter now.

4 Cook the pancakes over medium heat until they are browned on the bottom. Turn them over and continue cooking until browned on the other side. Remove from the pan and serve hot.

QUICK ᴵᴺ PAINLESS

One of the "recipes" suitable for preschool children is to let them peel string cheese (mozzarella) and put it on a plate with cut-up fruit or vegetables.

Bubble or Monkey Bread

Some kids call this bubble bread, some call it monkey bread because of its wrinkly "face." If you start with refrigerated bread dough or dough you've made in the bread machine, it's easy enough for even young children to make, as long as you melt the butter and bake the bread.

Older kids can make this recipe completely on their own.

- **Preparation Time:** 10 to 15 minutes
- **Baking Time:** 30 minutes
- **Servings:** 8

$^1/_3$ cup butter or margarine

1 egg, lightly beaten

1 tablespoon dried dill weed, or cilantro or parsley flakes

$^1/_2$ teaspoon garlic powder

1 loaf (1 pound) frozen bread dough (preferably whole wheat), thawed according to package directions

1. Preheat the oven to 375°F. Grease (or let your child grease) a disposable 8-by-3$^7/_8$-inch bread pan.

2. Put the butter in a small, microwave-proof bowl. Melt it in the microwave on high (100 percent) for 30 to 45 seconds, or just until melted. Mix in the egg, dill, and garlic powder.

3. Break off the dough in small, walnut-size pieces. Roll each piece of dough in the flavored butter and set the dough pieces in the loaf pan, stacking them on top of each other.

IF YOU'RE SO
INCLINED

If you have more than one child, you might want to let them make individual breads or rolls. They can put the dough in muffin cups or mini-bread pans.

4 Bake the bread in the center of the oven for 30 minutes, or until golden. Cool in the pan for 5 minutes, then, using potholders, turn the bread out of the pan onto a wire rack to finish cooling.

Raisin Cinnamon Bubble Bread: Follow the recipe, except omit the dill and garlic powder. Mix $\frac{1}{3}$ cup sugar with 2 teaspoons cinnamon. Roll the dough balls in the butter-egg mixture, then in the cinnamon sugar. As the child piles up the dough in the pan, have her sprinkle it with $\frac{1}{4}$ cup raisins.

YOU'LL THANK YOURSELF LATER

Use paper plates when kids help prepare foods, and disposable pans for baking. You'll save time in cleanup.

IF YOU'RE SO
INCLINED

If you like to cook, or have an older child who really likes to cook, consider investing in a hand-cranked pasta machine. Making pasta can be a lot of fun for kids, and fresh noodles are delicious.

Pink Pasta with Pesto

Kids over the age of 6 or 7 can toss the pasta with the beets and the sauce. Kids 10 to 12 can dump the pasta into the boiling water. Only teenagers should drain the pasta.

Preparation Time: about 10 minutes

Cooking Time: 5 to 7 minutes

Servings: 3 to 4

One 9-ounce package fresh fettuccini
2 teaspoons olive oil
One 15-ounce can julienne beets (don't drain)
One 7-ounce container refrigerated reduced-fat pesto

Cook the fettuccini according to the package directions. Drain.

While the pasta is cooking, drain the beets, saving the juice. Measure out ¼ cup of the beet juice and pour it into a large bowl. Add the oil. Put the beets aside, and throw away the rest of the beet juice.

Drain the pasta. Put it in the bowl and toss it gently with the beet juice until the pasta turns pink and has absorbed the juice. Add the pesto and toss to coat the pasta with it.

Divide the pasta among dinner plates. Spoon the julienne beets on top. Serve immediately.

Dorothy's Spaghetti Bread

Barbara, who contributed this recipe, said she and her kids invented this when the children were young and her daughter suggested tossing some leftover spaghetti into the bread dough. The results were delicious.

Younger kids can help grease the pan, mix the spaghetti into the dough, and sprinkle the bread with the cheese.

Preparation Time: About 8 minutes (not including dough defrosting)

Baking Time: About 30 minutes

Servings: 8

One 1-pound loaf frozen bread dough, preferably whole wheat, defrosted according to the package directions (or, use the breadmaker dough above)

$^1/_2$ cup leftover cooked spaghetti, with sauce

1 egg white, lightly beaten

$^1/_4$ cup grated fresh Parmesan cheese

1. Preheat the oven to 375°F. Grease or spray a disposable 8-by-3$^7/_8$-inch loaf pan.

2. Instruct the child to gently incorporate the spaghetti into the defrosted bread dough.

3. Set the dough in the prepared pan. Brush the top of the bread with the egg white and sprinkle it with the cheese.

4. Bake in the center of the oven for 30 minutes, or until the bread is golden and sounds hollow when tapped. Cool for 5 minutes, then turn the bread out of the pan onto a wire rack.

> The kids have been so good about helping out in the kitchen, why not reward them with some bauble they've had their heart set on, no matter how useless or silly you may think it is?

The Lazy Way

Getting Time on Your Side

	The Old way	**The Lazy way**
Mixing bread dough	20 minutes	5 minutes
Checking on the dough	10 minutes	Don't bother
Chopping chiles	5 minutes	0 minutes
Making pesto	10 minutes	0 minutes
Washing bread pans	5 minutes	Just toss it
Cooking for kids	30 minutes	Let them do it

Easy Treat

I remember once reading about a man whose mom used to make birthday cake, then scrape the frosting off before serving it. Too much fat, you know. Then there was the low-fat food maven who ordered a pizza and immediately picked off and discarded the cheese.

I have to wonder where these folks were when they were handing out the good humor (and I don't mean the ice cream bars). I'm all for nutrition, but is it really necessary to serve whole wheat crackers and broccoli for your son's birthday party?

Now, that doesn't mean the party has to be an all-out orgy of fat and refined sugar. Kids in America do get too much sugar and fat in their diets, and a little moderation here and there never hurt. Here are strategies for treating the kids and throwing parties without throwing time, and nutrition, completely out the door.

IT'S MY PARTY

It's your party and you can cry if you want to, but there is really no need. A little planning can make it a joyous affair.

Time-Saving Tips

Have It Somewhere Else

That way you do not have to clean house before the party, and again after the party. The drawback is that you probably won't get a wide choice of menu items, if the place even serves food.

If you have the party someplace where the kids can be active, such as an indoor playground or bowling alley, the kids can have some exercise with their fun. In the warm season, you might host a picnic in the park. You supply the food, but you still don't have to clean house.

Enlist a Helper

This can be your spouse, a neighbor, a teenager in the neighborhood who wants to earn a few bucks, or one of the other parents.

Keep the Structure Loose if the Kids Are Young

If your daughter's turning 3, the kids are just going to want to play and fight over toys. You can plan all sorts of elaborate little toddler games, and chances are you'll discard the whole idea 10 minutes into the party. Hire a clown, and they'll talk and scream through his show. The easiest plan for toddlers and preschoolers: Let them run, eat cake, and rip open the presents.

Have the Kids Make the Food

Kids over the age of 4 or 5 can help put together their own party. Put out pizza crusts and let them add the toppings. Let them assemble the Pretty-as-a-Picture Vegetable or Fruit Pizza (see recipe on page 206). You can even have the partygoers decorate the cake.

QUICK ⬭ PAINLESS

To make a very simple dessert for any party, cut slices of store-bought angel cake and top with a scoop of low-fat vanilla frozen yogurt, then with chopped canned or fresh pineapple, crushed strawberries or raspberries, or sliced peaches.

For older kids, you could even turn the party into a cooking lesson, complete with printed recipe cards. They'll probably be so tickled they won't notice they're doing all the work.

Even if It's Lunchtime, Forget the Real Food and Just Serve Snacks

Pretzels, raw veggies, popcorn (for older kids), and cut-up fruit with dips suit most kids fine. They're just going to fill up on the cake anyway.

Keeping It Nutritious (or at Least Not Too Bad)

- Make the cake low-fat and sneak some fruit puree into it. If the kids will go for it, banana cake or carrot cake both have above-average nutritional value.

- Serve the cake minus ice cream, or with reduced-fat ice cream or frozen yogurt.

- Order (or make) pizzas that are a bit lighter on the cheese.

- Serve reduced-fat chicken or turkey dogs.

- Serve pretzels instead of chips.

- Go ahead and serve some fruits and vegetables—but make sure there's some fun involved in preparing and eating them.

- Serve fruit juice or vitamin C–fortified fruit punch instead of soft drinks.

- Stuff the goodie bags with small toys and stickers, bubble gum (for kids 5 and above), and low-fat

IF YOU'RE SO
INCLINED

Make special ice cubes. Have your kids put a raspberry, a seedless grape (cut it in half for kids under 4), or a cube of melon in each ice cube compartment. Fill the tray with water or apple juice, and freeze.

treats such as lollipops or Sweet Tarts, Gummi Bears, or Tootsie Roll candies, rather than chocolate bars.

- Relax about the frosting.

There are some foods that just aren't paragons of good nutrition—butter cookies and frosting come immediately to mind. And scraping it off the cake is bound to earn you most-hated-parent award on the kiddie circuit, with good reason. You can buy reduced-fat frosting, but reduced-fat or not, frosting is basically nothing but sugar and some fat. Which, of course, is why kids adore it.

EFFORTLESS EVERYDAY SNACKING

Well, sure, parties are special occasions. But what about those day-to-day treats?

Snacks as Rewards

Every parent resorts to food rewards once in a while—"You can have your cupcake after you clean your room"—but it's best not to make a habit of it. You want your kid to view a cookie as just a cookie, and not the Holy Grail.

Nutritional Snacks

Try to choose sweet snacks that have some nutritional value. A nonfat chocolate cookie is still mostly sugar. Fruit, of course, is best sweet snack of all, but there also are cookies and other treats that provide more than fat and/or sugar: oatmeal cookies, molasses cookies, fig bars, sweetened cereals (especially the whole grain ones), and

YOU'LL THANK YOURSELF LATER

Be sure to include regular snack times in the daily routine. Kids get hungry between meals. And just like us, when they're grumpy and hungry, they often reach for fatty, sugary foods.

rice cakes, to name a few. For that matter, baby carrots taste nice and sweet to most kids.

Nuts and Peanuts

If your children are older (at least 6), nuts and peanuts make a good snack. They're rich in vitamins, minerals, and "good" fats, and they're very satisfying. Other savory choices include cereal snack mix, pretzels, and reduced-fat cheese crackers.

THE RECIPES

Standing at the stove for hours is probably pretty low on your list of things to do for your kid's birthday. But following are two kid-pleasers that require minimal preparation.

QUICK ⬭ PAINLESS

For older kids, put out an assortment of cut-up fruits, vegetables, cubes of cheese, and toothpicks. Have them build silly food structures with the whole lot.

So the birthday girl has changed her mind and is begging for chocolate cake—after you bought a yellow cake mix? Don't run to the store. Just add 6 tablespoons of unsweetened cocoa powder to the mix, and increase the amount of water by $^1/_4$ cup.

Homemade Chocolate Baking Mix

There's nothing wrong with cake mixes, and you can make them lower in fat by simply substituting applesauce or apricot baby food for the oil. But your own cake mix not only tastes better, but can serve as a baking lesson. Your child can help you measure and stir.

- **Preparation Time:** 5 to 10 minutes
- **Servings:** Makes about 5 cups (enough for 36 cup-cakes or two 13-by-9-inch cakes)

$1^1/_2$ cups sugar
3 cups all-purpose flour
$^1/_2$ cup unsweetened cocoa powder
3 teaspoons baking powder
1 teaspoon salt

1   In a large bowl, whisk together the sugar, flour, cocoa, baking powder, and salt until well mixed.

2   Divide the mix evenly into three resealable plastic storage bags. (You should have a scant $1^3/_4$ cups per bag.) Squeeze out as much air as possible, seal the bag tightly, and store in a dry, cool cupboard for up to six months.

Chocolate Cupcakes with White Frosting

Preparation Time: 10 minutes

Baking Time: 20 minutes

Servings: 12 cupcakes

1 package of Homemade Chocolate Baking Mix (about 1^3/$_4$ cups); see recipe on page 204

2 eggs

^{1}/$_3$ cup light mayonnaise

^{3}/$_4$ to 1 cup skim milk, or enough to make a smooth batter

One 16-ounce can white frosting

Chocolate or colored sprinkles (optional)

1. Preheat the oven to 350°F. Line a 12-cup muffin tin with paper cupcake liners.

2. In a mixing bowl, combine the baking mix, eggs, mayonnaise, and milk. Beat the batter on medium speed for 2 minutes. Spoon the batter into the prepared pan.

3. Bake in the middle of the oven for about 20 minutes or until a knife inserted in the center of a cupcake comes out clean.

4. Let the cupcakes stay in the pan for 5 minutes, then turn them out and cool on a wire rack.

5. When the cupcakes are cool, spread with frosting and decorate with sprinkles. Serve.

Variation: Instead of the mayonnaise, use 2 tablespoons melted butter or margarine and ^{1}/$_3$ cup applesauce (or a 5-ounce jar of apricot or prune baby food).

YOU'LL THANK YOURSELF LATER

Baking powder loses its potency after a while. Look at the expiration date (it's usually on the bottom of the can), and scrawl it in marker on the side of the can. That way you're more likely to remember to toss it and buy a new can if necessary.

Pretty-as-a-Picture Vegetable or Fruit Pizza

This is a variation on a popular party recipe for adults. Make sure you have different shaped fruit and vegetable pieces, so the kids can get creative.

Preparation Time: 20 to 25 minutes

Baking Time: 10 minutes

Servings: 12 to 14

Two 8-ounce cans crescent rolls

12 ounces light cream cheese, softened

An assortment of cut-up raw fruits and/or vegetables: broccoli florets, red pepper slices, sliced cucumbers, sliced olives, alfalfa sprouts, snap peas, sliced or grated carrots or carrot sticks; melon cubes, strawberries, blueberries, raisins, halved grapes, banana or apple slices (sprinkle them with lemon juice)

1. Preheat the oven to 400°F.

2. Unroll the crescent roll dough and lay the pieces evenly over a 10-by-15-inch jelly-roll pan, pressing with your fingers to eliminate any seams between the dough pieces. Prick with a fork in several places.

3. Bake in the center of the oven for 10 minutes, or until golden. Remove to a wire rack, and let the crust cool completely.

4. Spread the cream cheese evenly over the crust. Cover the crust loosely with plastic wrap and refrigerate it until serving time.

QUICK n' PAINLESS

For a quick lunch, snack, or party food, make potato cakes with a surprise inside. Cook frozen hash browns until very crisp. Just before serving, place a slice of cheese in the center. Roll the hash browns up (use a napkin so you don't burn your fingers) with the cheese inside, and serve.

5　The day of the party, cut up all the fruits and/or vegetables, put on festive paper plates, and refrigerate.

6　At the party, set out the plates of cut-up fruits and/or vegetables, and let the kids arrange them over the crust to make pretty pictures.

7　Cut into squares, and serve.

Variation: If the kids are under 6, and therefore more likely to fight than cooperate, you can have them make individual picture pizzas, using English muffins, pita breads, or even several crackers shoved together.

You've survived, and the birthday party was a noisy success. If there's someone to spell you, sneak out for a quiet, solo walk.

The Lazy Way

Getting Time on Your Side

	The Old Way	The Lazy Way
Scraping frosting off cake	5 minutes	Don't do it
Planning toddler games	2 hours	Don't bother
Making a cake from scratch	30 minutes	5 minutes
Serving lunch at the party	30 minutes	10 minutes
Switching from yellow to chocolate cake	1 hour	5 minutes
Cleaning up after the party	1 hour	Let somebody else do it

More Lazy Stuff

How to Get Someone Else to Do It

There are going to be times—probably quite a few times—when you just plain do not want to cook. Your spouse doesn't want to cook. Your kids don't want to cook. The cat doesn't know how to cook, and wouldn't stoop to such a chore even if she did.

So, how do you get someone else to cook for you? No problem! Here are some tips for taking it easy:

Live in a Big City
The trade-off for living in an overcrowded metropolis is that you do not have to drive, or even walk, anywhere to get food. You pick up the phone, give your address, and soon have Chinese food, pizza, gourmet carryout, Italian pasta, bagels, you name it, right at your front door.

You can get delivery in smaller cities, too, but your choices are a bit more limited. Unless you live in the country, you can always get pizza. Order it with a vegetable topping, and light on the cheese.

Carry It Out
If you don't live in a city where you can get everything including the kitchen sink delivered, you'll have to get in the car and go get it.

Fortunately, nearly every restaurant, short of the four- and five-star dining establishments, will let you get food to go.

By the way, don't toss nutrition out the window just because someone else is cooking. The easiest way to keep the grease in check is to think veggies and starch: lo mein, rice, bread, pasta with a tomato sauce, chicken-vegetable soup, pizza that's easy on the cheese, baked potatoes, bean burritos, the small burger (it's more bun than meat), corn, fruit salad.

Have the Supermarket Come to You

In many cities (and not just the largest ones), you can have groceries delivered, usually for a fairly reasonable fee. Some supermarkets even have online ordering. Call your supermarket to see if they offer this service.

Try to Avoid the Drive-Thru

When's the last time you ordered a reasonably low-fat, nutritious meal from a fast-food drive-thru? I rest my case.

Hire a Chef

It's not just for rich folks with servants anymore. Personal chefs shop, plan menus, and prepare meals for your family, usually at a reasonable cost. Usually, one personal chef serves several families, and prepares nutritious meals that you can reheat after work. To find a chef in your area, contact the United States Personal Chef Association, (800) 995-2138. If you visit the association's Web Site, www.uspca.com, you can look up chefs in your area and e-mail questions to them.

Look Beyond the Kids' Menu in Restaurants

Many of them feature little besides burgers, hot dogs, fries, and grilled cheese. There's no law that says you can't order your kid a turkey sandwich, a bowl of soup, or a shrimp cocktail. You can always take home any leftovers.

On the other hand, in the big burger chains you're pretty much stuck with the kids' meals for a simple reason: They come with toys. You're not going to talk your child into a salad when it doesn't come with the latest Disney doodad.

Realize There Are Times when Nutrition Simply Has to Take a Backseat

When you're planning your child's birthday party, for example, you may want to have it somewhere besides your house, like a fast-food restaurant with party accommodations, or an indoor playground. Except for the cake, you're stuck eating whatever food they serve. Which is probably burgers and fries, hot dogs and chips, or pizza. If you have the choice, go with pizza, which at least offers some calcium and what passes for a vegetable.

Make Use of the School Lunch Program

Bless those school lunches, which can save you from the drudgery of making one peanut butter or turkey sandwich after another. Now you just have to hope the school has decent food and your kid likes it. Many schools have breakfast programs as well. These can be a lifesaver if you have a very hectic schedule or need to get to work very early in the morning. If your school offers weekly or monthly lunch "tickets," use them; it's easier for you and your child to remember lunch money once a week than every day.

B

If You Really Want More, Read These

There are plenty of good resources out there related to children's nutrition. Here are a few of my favorites.

BOOKS

If you have trouble finding any of these books in a bookstore, check your local library.

Jennings, Debbi Sowell, and Suzanne Nelson Steen. *Play Hard, Eat Right: A Parents' Guide to Sports Nutrition for Children.* Chronimed, 1995.

This book by two dietitians explores the issues of nutrition for recreational and competitive athletes ages 6 to 12. It includes recipes for healthful meals and snacks.

Lansky, Vicki. *Feed Me! I'm Yours.* Meadowbrook Press, 1994.

This longtime parents' favorite focuses on feeding babies and young children and features more than 200 recipes.

Laskin, David. *Parents Book of Child Safety*. Ballantine, 1991.

General information on making your home and environment safe for children, including information on kitchen and food safety.

Messina, Virginia and Mark Messina. *The Vegetarian Way: Total Health for You and Your Family*. Crown, 1996.

An excellent introduction to vegetarianism. Includes chapters on healthful vegetarian diets for children, from infancy through the teen years.

Satter, Ellyn. *How to Get Your Kid to Eat...But Not Too Much*. Bull Publishing, 1987.

———. *Child of Mine: Feeding With Love and Good Sense*. Bull Publishing, 1991.

Both of these books are classics in the field of child nutrition. *How to Get Your Kid to Eat...But Not Too Much* offers strategies for kids ranging from babies through teenagers. *Child of Mine* focuses on babies and toddlers, and shares tips and insights for pregnant women and new parents. These aren't recipe books; they focus on child development and the psychology of eating.

MAGAZINES

Zillions

Consumer Reports' bimonthly magazine for kids 8 and up is a general consumer guide, but often includes articles on food and nutrition, and is useful in helping children figure out how advertisers target them. A subscription costs $16 a year: P.O. Box 54861, Boulder, CO 80322-4861.

WEB SITES

Kids Food CyberClub

http://www.kidsfood.org/

A great site for kids. It includes learning activities, kids' recipes, a scavenger hunt, a "rate your plate" guide to food groups and servings, food facts, and information about gardening and hunger. It also includes sections for parents and teachers. It's sponsored by the Connecticut Association for Human Services and funded by Kaiser Permanente.

Dole 5 a Day

http://www.dole5aday.com

This lively site from the Dole Food Company encourages kids to eat five daily servings of fruits and vegetables. It features games, nutritional information, resources for parents and teachers, and a kids' cookbook.

Broccoli Town

http://www.broccoli.com

This site features games, a history of broccoli, and recipes. It's sponsored by Mann Packing Company, which sells packaged produce, such as broccoli and snap peas.

CSPI Chow Club

http://www.cspinet.org

Center for Science in the Public Interest's section for kids includes basic nutritional information and recipes.

Parent Soup

http://www.parentsoup.com

Village's excellent parenting section has various nutrition-related articles scattered throughout, including information on family nutrition and vegetarianism.

American Dietetic Association

http://www.eatright.org

ADA is the professional organization for dietitians. The site offers fact sheets, position papers, and other publications related to over-all nutrition and some specific to children's nutrition.

Nutrition for Children

http://www.teleport.com/~eversc/NFC.htm

The site for 24 Carrot Press, which publishes teaching materials on children's nutrition, includes the excellent "Feeding Kids" newsletter, suitable for teachers, parents, and kids.

U.S. Food and Drug Administration's Center for Food Safety and Applied Nutrition

http://vm.cfsan.fda.gov/list.html

Includes a variety of nutrition- and food safety–related topics, including information on food labeling and additives.

Four Simple Steps to Fight Bac!

http://www.fightbac.org

Sponsored by the Partnership for Food Safety Education. Offers food handling and cooking information to help you ward off bacteria that can make you sick.

U.S. Department of Agriculture's Food and Nutrition Information Center

http://www.nalusda.gov/fnic/

The USDA regulates meats, poultry, and eggs, and the federal school meal program. The site features varied nutrition information, and a graphic of the agency's Food Guide Pyramid.

Composition of Foods

http://www.nal.usda.gov/fnic/foodcomp/

Want to know the calories, fats, vitamins, and minerals in a particular food? The USDA now has its searchable food database online.

If You Don't Know What It Means, Look Here

Calcium: An essential mineral required for building strong bones and teeth. Milk and other dairy products are the most popular sources for the mineral. Other excellent sources include canned salmon and calcium-fortified orange juice. Vegetable sources of calcium include bok choy and broccoli. Having enough vitamin D helps the body absorb calcium. Children and young women have the greatest need for calcium.

Carbohydrates: A wide range of foods, such as vegetables, fruits, and bread, that supply energy to your body. Starches and dietary fiber are complex carbohydrates; fruits, vegetables, and grains are good examples. Sugars are simple carbohydrates. Most foods have both kinds, but complex carbohydrates are the kinds your kids should eat the most.

Cholesterol: People think it's bad. But your body makes this waxy substance, which is essential for digesting fats, and forming sex hormones, digestive juices, and vitamin D. It's important in the structure of brain and nerve cells, which is why doctors warn against putting children under the age of 2 on a low-fat, low-cholesterol diet. High blood cholesterol normally isn't a problem in children, unless they have really lousy diets or there's a family history of elevated cholesterol. Cholesterol is found in all animal foods, including eggs, meats, poultry, seafood, and dairy products.

Copper: An essential mineral that helps your body absorb and use iron and form red blood cells. It also helps the nervous system function normally. Kid-friendly sources of copper include nuts, mushrooms, sweet potatoes, potatoes, dried beans, pears, and tofu. If your child's copper intake is low, his iron absorption also decreases, which could lead to anemia.

Fat: Officially, it's a substance composed of three fatty acids and glycerol, generally called a triglyceride. Unofficially, it's the stuff that makes food greasy. Fats contain saturated, monounsaturated, and polyunsaturated fatty acids. Hydrogenated oils (such as margarine and shortening) can contain fairly high amounts of trans fatty acids as well. Your body does need some fat, and babies and toddlers need a fairly high amount of it, which is why you should not restrict fat in a very young child's diet. Experts recommend that adults and kids over the age of 5 get 30 percent or less of their calories from fat, and no more than 10 percent from saturated fat. Current research indicates that trans fats may act much like saturated fat in the body. The best way to keep fat moderate in your kids' diet is to serve nonfat or reduced-fat dairy products; lean meats and poultry without the skin, and fewer full-fat baked goods.

Fiber: More accurately called dietary fiber, this is a collection of naturally occurring, nondigestible substances found mostly in plant foods. Fruits, vegetables, seeds, nuts, and whole grains are the best sources of fiber. For children, the recommendation for fiber is to add the age plus 5 grams a day, so a 9-year-old should get 14 grams of fiber. Fiber has many benefits, but one obvious one in kids is that it helps keep them from getting constipated.

Folate: This B vitamin may help prevent neural-tube defects (such as spina bifida) in babies. Grain products are now fortified with folate to ensure that Americans, especially women of childbearing age, get enough of the vitamin. Folate may also be good for the heart. Rich sources include dark green, leafy vegetables; oranges, and dried beans and peas.

Iron: An essential mineral that transports oxygen through the blood to all parts of your body. Iron also plays an important role in the immune system, and having low iron levels can lower your child's resistance to infection. Fatigue and weakness are symptoms of iron deficiency. Low iron levels are most common among babies (over 6 months) and toddlers, and teenage girls and young women. Iron from animal sources tends to be better absorbed than iron from plant foods. However, vitamin C helps your body better absorb iron. Red meats, dried fruit, and dried beans and peas are good to excellent sources. An overdose of iron can be life-threatening to young children, so always keep iron supplements well out of their reach.

Magnesium: A mineral required by all cells. Your body needs it for a wide range of functions, including building bone, breaking down carbohydrates, and keeping the heart functioning. Good sources include artichokes, beans, whole grains, and shellfish.

Manganese: A trace mineral that helps the body form connective tissue and bones, and aids in metabolism. Good sources of manganese include nuts, seeds, whole grains, and pineapple.

Niacin: Also called vitamin B_3, it helps in the release of energy from carbohydrates; aids in the breakdown of protein and fats, and helps form red blood cells and maintain all body cells. Fatty fish (like salmon), tuna, chicken, pork, and peanuts are all rich in niacin.

Phosphorus: An essential mineral that helps enzymes function and aids various chemical reactions in your body. Phosphorus is widely available from dairy products, meat, cereal grains, and fish. Calcium and phosphorus work together in the body. Getting too much phosphorus and not enough calcium could result in bone loss.

Potassium: A mineral that helps keep a proper level of fluids in your body. It helps to regulate blood pressure and heart function, and to transmit nerve impulses. Bananas are a popular choice for potassium, but many foods, including apricots, avocados, beans, potatoes, and yogurt, provide excellent amounts.

Protein: Ask any schoolkid—protein is the "building block of nutrition." The body breaks it down into amino acids, which it uses to build brain tissue, muscles, blood and skin; to repair tissues; and to create antibodies, enzymes, and hormones. The American diet is high in protein, so a deficiency is unusual. Good sources of protein for kids include lean meats and poultry, low-fat milk, beans, wheat, and peanut butter.

Riboflavin: A substance sometimes referred to as vitamin B_2, riboflavin is necessary for the growth and repair of tissues and is found in every cell of your body. Good sources include milk and dairy products, and fish and seafood.

Selenium: An essential trace mineral that helps protect red blood cells from damage. Whole grain foods, such as brown rice, wheat germ, and whole wheat bread, can be especially good sources. Seafood is also very rich in selenium. Selenium can be toxic in large amounts.

Thiamin; thiamine: A substance, also called vitamin B_1, that your body needs to metabolize carbohydrates and keep your nervous system stable. Thiamin is most abundant in pork and nuts.

Vitamin A: A substance you need for growth, good vision, immune system strength, and maintenance of cells. Preformed vitamin A comes from animal sources such as liver and fish oils, but most "vitamin A" actually comes from carotenoids, such as beta carotene, found in plant foods such as dark leafy greens, carrots, sweet potatoes, hard-shell squash, apricots, and cantaloupe. Your body turns these carotenoids into vitamin A.

Vitamin B_1: See Thiamin.

Vitamin B$_2$: See Riboflavin.

Vitamin B$_3$: See Niacin.

Vitamin B$_6$: A family of compounds that your body needs to metabolize carbohydrates, fat, and protein. It might also help keep the immune system in shape. Vitamin B$_6$ is widely available in foods such as poultry, fish, whole grains, and bananas.

Vitamin B$_{12}$: A compound that your body needs to process carbohydrates, proteins, and fats, and to make nerve sheaths. Vitamin B$_{12}$ is available from animal sources. Shellfish is a rich source. Vegetarians can get it from fortified cereals or vitamin supplements. A deficiency of vitamin B$_{12}$ can result in a serious form of anemia.

Vitamin C: A substance that helps the body form collagen in connective tissue, aids in the healing of wounds, and helps keep the immune system healthy. Vitamin C helps reduce iron to a form your body can use. Heat can destroy vitamin C, and it's best to get it from fresh raw foods. Good sources include citrus fruits, strawberries, kiwifruit, tomatoes, bell peppers, cabbage, and papayas. A lot of juices and juice drinks also are fortified with C. Bleeding gums and frequent, slow-healing bruises could mean your child is deficient in this vitamin.

Vitamin D: A fat-soluble vitamin necessary for bone formation. Your body makes it from sunlight, but fortified milk is a good source for kids as well. If your children play outdoors in the sun and drink milk, don't give them vitamin D supplements; it's toxic in large amounts.

Vitamin E: A family of compounds that help protect cells from damage. For kids, good sources include vegetable oils, peanut butter, mayonnaise, nuts, and sunflower seeds.

Vitamin K: A substance that's essential for blood clotting and may also help your body form bone. Green and leafy green vegetables such as broccoli and kale, are all rich sources of vitamin K.

Zinc: A trace mineral that's involved in several metabolic processes, such as the breakdown of carbohydrates. Zinc plays a role in immune system function, the replication of genetic material, sexual development, and the normal activity of your taste buds. Zinc-rich foods include meat and dark-meat poultry.

D

It's Time for Your Reward

Once You've Done This:	Reward Yourself:
Cooked four nights in a row	With a home-delivered meal
Cleaned the kitchen	With a soak in the tub
Organized the kitchen	With a slice of warm bread and fancy jam
Fed your kids a nutritious dinner	With a favorite movie
Chopped and prepared ingredients ahead of time	And your kids with an exotic-fruit tasting
Survived shopping with your kids	And your kids with a goofy activity like chasing grasshoppers
Pulled off a successful birthday party	With a solo walk

Index

Now you can do these tasks, too!

Starting to think there are a few more of life's little tasks that you've been putting off? Don't worry—we've got you covered. Take a look at all of *The Lazy Way* books available. Just imagine—you can do almost anything *The Lazy Way!*

Clean Your House The Lazy Way
By Barbara H. Durham
0-02-862649-4

Handle Your Money The Lazy Way
By Sarah Young Fisher and Carol Turkington
0-02-862632-X

Care for Your Home The Lazy Way
By Terry Meany
0-02-862646-X

Train Your Dog The Lazy Way
By Andrea Arden
0-87605180-8

Take Care of Your Car The Lazy Way
By Michael Kennedy and Carol Turkington
0-02-862647-8

Learn Spanish The Lazy Way
By Vivian Isaak and Bogumila Michalewicz
0-02-862650-8

*All Lazy Way books are just $12.95!

additional titles on the back!

Build Your Financial Future The Lazy Way
By Terry Meany
0-02-862648-6

Shed Some Pounds The Lazy Way
By Annette Cain and Becky Cortopassi-Carlson
0-02-862999-X

Organize Your Stuff The Lazy Way
By Toni Ahlgren
0-02-863000-9

Cook Your Meals The Lazy Way
By Sharon Bowers
0-02-862644-3

Cut Your Spending The Lazy Way
By Leslie Haggin
0-02-863002-5

Stop Aging The Lazy Way
By Judy Myers, Ph.D.
0-02-862793-8

Get in Shape The Lazy Way
By Annette Cain
0-02-863010-6

Learn French The Lazy Way
By Christophe Desmaison
0-02-863011-4

Learn Italian The Lazy Way
By Gabrielle Euvino
0-02-863014-9

Keep Your Kids Busy The Lazy Way
By Barbara Nielsen and Patrick Wallace
0-02-863013-0